POSITIVE PSYCHOLOGY OF LEARNING AND DEVELOPMENT

HOW TO CULTIVATE A LEARNING CULTURE THAT ENTAILS INCORPORATING LEARNING INTO BUSINESS OBJECTIVES IN DAY-TO-DAY OPERATIONS?

DR. AMIT DAS

Copyright © Dr. Amit Das
All Rights Reserved.

This book has been published with all efforts taken to make the material error-free after the consent of the author. However, the author and the publisher do not assume and hereby disclaim any liability to any party for any loss, damage, or disruption caused by errors or omissions, whether such errors or omissions result from negligence, accident, or any other cause.

While every effort has been made to avoid any mistake or omission, this publication is being sold on the condition and understanding that neither the author nor the publishers or printers would be liable in any manner to any person by reason of any mistake or omission in this publication or for any action taken or omitted to be taken or advice rendered or accepted on the basis of this work. For any defect in printing or binding the publishers will be liable only to replace the defective copy by another copy of this work then available.

To

All my bosses and mentors who made a difference in my professional career.

"Most businesses do not provide their employees—especially managers—the tools they need to take charge of their own growth. These people are now left helpless and unsure of what to do in their future course of action. Organisations that have reduced their use of in-person experiential learning have not conducted enough research to determine which demands call for this kind of learning and which may be adequately met by only granting access to information or learning. The general belief in most organisations seems to be that everyone will become highly proficient if we make enough learning materials freely available. In conclusion, it may be necessary for the development pendulum to swing back to incorporate more intentional investment in real development as opposed to just learning."

- Dr. Amit Das, Motivational Speaker, Counsellor, Leadership Coach and Mentor.

Contents

Foreword

"We now accept the fact that learning is a lifelong process of keeping abreast of change. And the most pressing task is to teach people how to learn."- Peter Drucker

Dear Readers,

Thank you for taking the time to learn more about organisational transformation through its learning and the rewarding outcome of increased employee engagement and productivity. The company's overall employee learning agility as well as job engagement will be impacted by the learning culture that is created. Management can use a culture map as a compass to guide corporate culture toward a learning culture. Over the past two years, there have been significant changes in the way you work, and this is only the beginning. You are frequently left wondering how to establish a culture where workers are content and fulfilled in their jobs as organisations grow more sensitive to their requirements and as people become more outspoken about their wants.

More than just offering learning or training sessions, cultivating a learning culture entails incorporating learning into the business's objectives and daily operations. In this book, learning strategist Dr. Amit Das outlines the duties that each individual in the organisation—from L&D and HR specialists to managers and leaders to the employees themselves—should play in fostering this culture. In order to assist you in creating and implementing a learning programme, the author provides best practises. Additionally, he covers some of the challenges organisations may encounter during the process and offers tips and techniques to assist you in becoming more competitive in your particular markets and fostering a culture of learning.

This book, "Positive Psychology Of Learning And Development" and its strategy, evidence, and practice, gives a thorough and topical review of the theories, scientific findings, and applications of strategic L&D in organisations. It covers both strategic and operational practise dimensions to aid HRM and learning and development professionals or students in developing a thorough understanding of the field.

" Sustainable learning culture tend to put people in charge of their own learning through programme like personalised development plans, learning that happens naturally while doing work, and technology that enables learning at any time, anywhere. This has the potential to become a self-fulfilling prophecy over time, when learners actively seek out information and learning takes on a life of its own."

The author of this book uses a wide range of academic perspectives to examine the history and current use of organisational learning. It critically examines organisational knowledge's social constructional character, pedagogical concerns about how people, groups, teams, and entire organisations learn, and technological concerns about how knowledge-based information systems are created. The book includes supporting real-world examples, and readers will also gain much from this book. Readers of "Positive Psychology Of Learning And Development" will be able to create and put into practise plans for assuring ongoing access to an organisation's ingrained knowledge and experience. This book will be an excellent resource for management students, HR professionals, and learning professionals.

"Science is both a body of knowledge and a process. Art is the expression of creativity and imagination. Where they intersect is the best way to help others learn and grow."

Your organisation already has a learning culture, whether you realise it or not. Because humans are inherently designed to learn and do so every day, every business does this. The true question is whether your organisation is moving toward ever-higher levels of performance and success thanks to your learning culture. The author will focus on how to deliberately establish a learning culture that is important to your organisation in this book. All sorts of leaders, from senior managers to intermediate managers, and from HR chiefs to trainers of all varieties and degrees, should read this book. While the emphasis of this book is on professional development, not only for you, educational institutions can also benefit from many of the same ideas. It also serves to guide the work of L&D professionals by identifying the best research on L&D practises and by giving them guidelines for action. The emphasis is on the contribution of L&D to organisational and financial success as well as the necessity of coordinating formal and informal L&D with corporate goals.

One issue that learning professionals frequently voice to me is that they are not given a place at the table. They aren't even consulted while making a strategic choice at the highest level of the company. This is partially due to their failure to frame learning as an organisational competitive advantage. The author believes that learning is a competitive edge that businesses may use to their benefit. This book demonstrates how to establish L&D as a valuable partner for your business, enhancing output, client interactions, and corporate skills. During your time reading this book, you'll learn how to enable your company to succeed. The author will work with you to assess the current learning culture you have in place and to make the transition to a powerful, deliberate culture of learning that will offer your business a competitive edge.

Also included in neuroscience for learning are observations from L&D professionals who have used these strategies. In addition to learning new strategies they can use right now, readers will learn about research that supports the things they are currently doing effectively, helping them to make compelling arguments to budget holders. This book provides L&D and training professionals with a knowledge of the inner workings of the mind by introducing the most recent research and concepts. It builds on the fundamental operational building blocks of L&D and extends beyond them to adopt a strategic approach. Each chapter includes real-world examples that help students or professionals apply concepts to workplace situations, make connections between theory and practise, and direct readers to the finest research on L&D methods.

Are you genuinely seeing results from your learning and development programme?

The author of this book delves deeply into this complex subject, explaining how to utilise learner, programme, and learning experience analytics to gauge your L&D effectiveness. This book redefines learning analytics for the digital era. The author examines the state of learning analytics today and talks about the moral repercussions of using big data to guide your learning and development plan. Additionally, the author contrasts various applications and approaches for learning analytics and looks ahead to its future. At the conclusion of this book, you will have a better understanding of how to apply learning analytics to discover fresh insights for your business. The author of this book, shares examples from his own experience as he discusses how to collect data, define and assess the learning experience, how learner evaluation may guide talent development, and other topics.

According to the author, organisations with strong learning cultures routinely outperform their competitors in terms of revenue growth, profitability, market share, and customer satisfaction.

> *"Whatever sustainability means to your team, sustainable learning cultures have a few universal characteristics that will help you succeed in the future."*

According to the author, other characteristics of sustainable learning cultures include tightly matched business and learning strategies; organisational values that uphold the value of learning; and a setting where learning is so pervasive that it simply becomes a way of life. Sustainability is becoming a crucial factor in numerous aspects of life, including L&D. This applies to economic sustainability, environmental sustainability, and the maintenance of a good work-life balance. In fact, developing a sustainable learning culture should be a major focus for L&D teams moving ahead, given the shortening of skill lifespans and the ongoing cycle of unlearning and relearning. The majority of HR leaders concur that creating a strong learning culture is the key to attaining successful business results and successfully addressing the changing nature of the workforce.

Assuring your team's goals will still be relevant in five years, safeguarding L&D's position in the global marketplace, or upskilling staff to preserve relevant abilities in a changing L&D landscape are all examples of what sustainability might mean to various L&D teams.

Learning analytics may assist you on both counts. It may enable you to connect the program's outcomes to your company's business objectives and highlight strengths and opportunities for both your programme and the learners you're trying to target.

Are you interested in learning how to develop personnel, increase customer happiness, and provide excellent performance?

With the influence of disruptive technological innovations on the competitive environment, a new generation of workers wanting more involvement and purpose, and shifting consumer expectations, the demand for organisations to transform is stronger than ever. organisations and their executives must have the skills to address these brand-new possibilities and challenges or they risk falling behind. Leadership that can push team members to discover and implement fresh ideas for action improvement through constant action is necessary for adapting.

The book provides useful tools and ideas that can be applied in a variety of contexts, from digital learning and in-person learning sessions, to coaching conversations, to lectures. It covers topics like how to create effective learning environments, promoting employee motivation and engagement, and how to make learning "stickier" through the use of technology. This book is what you need if you need to grasp anything you want to know about instructional content creation; it is interesting, comprehensive, and necessary. It offers just the appropriate mix of scholarly support, useful guidance, and perceptive design recommendations to have you quickly developing effective learning.

This book, "Positive Psychology Of Learning And Development," offers a useful foundation for use by HR, L&D, and OD professionals. No matter the size of the organisation, it outlines the steps involved in designing and delivering a successful learning and development function. It also ensures business alignment and offers a set of templates that may be used as-is or customised to meet user needs or guide system design. The story provides information on the strategic components, from theory and instructional design to implementation and return on investment; skills development, from needs analysis to delivery, assessment, and reporting; professional development and the advancement of skills, knowledge, or competence to operate in a professional capacity; and leadership development, which builds on workplace and professional skills to enable effective people and operations management. It critically examines organisational knowledge's social constructional character, pedagogical concerns about how people, groups, teams, and entire organisations learn, and technological concerns about how knowledge-based information systems are created. This book will assist learning or HR professionals in approaching and aligning their digital transformation, people strategy, and employee experience to promote long-term sustainability.

"Train people well enough so they can not leave, treat tem well enough so that they don't want to."- Richard Branson

Thank you for taking the time to read this book.

So, happy reading and learning to all my readers.

Carpe diem.

Dr. Amit Das

Preface

"Information is a source of learning. But unless it is organised, processed, and available to the right people in a format for decision making, it is a burden, not a benefit."

A learning organisation is one that is adept at knowledge creation, acquisition, and transfer as well as behaviour modification to take into account fresh information and insights. This concept starts with a fundamental truth: for learning to occur, new ideas are necessary.

A sustained learning culture has obvious benefits if, like me, you think that learning should never stop. To put it another way, teams that foster sustainable learning cultures also frequently have more success in terms of income, growth, and talent retention. Linking work-based training with an organisation's strategic goals and objectives may dramatically improve business performance and, critically, establish an organisational culture that promotes creativity, here I explain the strategic value of having a sustainable learning culture. By joining me, you will learn how to link corporate strategic initiatives to learning and development activities.

Does your learning organisation make use of data's potential?

Learning analytics is entering a new age with the introduction of big data, elearning, and a renewed focus on user experience. Businesses have traditionally evaluated the effectiveness of their L&D programmes. One in ten businesses doesn't use the information they gather. Perhaps this is related to the fact that 45% of L&D professionals claimed they are unsure of where to begin when it comes to data analysis for learning purposes. You must be able to interpret the growing amount of data available and apply it to enhance the learning process. You are losing out if you are not employing learning analytics. I'll cover several important subjects related to learning analytics in this book, such as what it is and how it works. The use of learning analytics will fundamentally alter how you approach learning.

I'll start by describing what constitutes a fantastic learning culture and the kinds of advantages it may provide. I'll also discuss the importance of the growth mindset and how to employ different instructional strategies to encourage lifelong learning. I'll demonstrate how various community members contribute to and own creating a culture of learning. I'll give you a brief summary of some recommended techniques and emerging fashions. Finally, I'll demonstrate how to overcome some typical roadblocks and how to assess the effectiveness of your efforts.

In the business, learning culture has a positive and considerable effect on organisational adaptability. The ability to adapt and innovate is positively and significantly impacted by a culture that values flexibility or development. An innovative corporate culture significantly and favourably affects the company's strategic adaptability. While a corporate culture that is hierarchical, such as bureaucratic, rigid with the rules, and one-directional from top to bottom, diminishes the effect of absorbency on organisational agility, a company culture that is efficiency-focused has little impact on strategic agility.

Learning is a continuous process. When entering the workplace, employees expect comprehensive L&D, and firms must be ready to provide this need. However, it's not just about retention rates or employee satisfaction scores.

To increase employee productivity, boost workplace happiness, and close critical gaps, Learning management teams must take the lead in transforming the learning culture. This book guides you through each step of the procedure, from putting tried-and-true tactics into practise to transforming event-based training.

"In any organisation, learning serves as the cornerstone for excellent execution, creativity, and innovation."

This book outlines the ways in which L&D teams might employ informal learning to supplement, assist, and reinforce official training programmes.

How can the L&D team transform event-based training into a continuous learning ecosystem?

Traditional training that focuses on a large number of discrete and unrelated events is ineffective and unable to foster a culture of learning. In this part, I outline how implementing a continuous learning process might enhance the way knowledge is applied and result in a shift in behaviour.

Too many learning initiatives fall flat. This book will discuss how companies can foster a culture of learning and invest in the skills necessary for both people and organisations to prosper. The majority of enterprises had the chance to optimise their business operations during the last 24 months. Organisations have reevaluated their digital strategies, goods, and services, scaled up operations, and found new market possibilities during this time. They have also optimised their talent plans.

"A workplace culture that encourages continuous learning and is nimble, adaptive, and resilient lies at the core of these developments."

Setting realistic expectations is essential for the effectiveness of learning and development. Stakeholders may have widely divergent opinions about the spending plan, the structure, or even the objectives of your programme, so it's critical to establish the facts up front. This book provides advice and methods that can assist you in controlling expectations and gaining support for your initiative. Learn how to respond to inquiries regarding costs, evaluate the effectiveness of training, justify the use of internal as opposed to external training providers, and offer reasonable time estimates for developing the training. Additionally, I will assist you in comprehending the proper reporting of employee engagement and promote strategies for generating and maintaining interest in your L&D programme.

"L&D helps businesses increase productivity, customer satisfaction, and their bottom line. However, a lot of L&D professionals don't believe they contribute to the success of their company."

Promote the value of training by portraying L&D as a competitive advantage and aligning it with your organisation's strategic goals in order to win over executives and boost employee engagement. In this book, I'll explain how to evaluate the program's maturity, articulate the benefits of a successful L&D department, and link learning objectives to corporate strategy. Additionally, find out how to gauge the accomplishment of your L&D programme using important learning measures and business objectives.

Neuroscience indicates that there are tried-and-true methods of persuasion that anybody can employ, despite the fact that success in persuasion sometimes seems to depend on charm, good fortune, or timing. Before you can start assisting others in their learning, you must have the knowledge and abilities necessary to effectively communicate information. Learn in this book how to train people in the modern corporate climate. I'll discuss methods and approaches for delivering effective workplace training that improves learner results.

I'll talk about creating, organising, and delivering effective training sessions as well as how to improve your communication skills and get through learning obstacles. The skills you learn in this book can improve your public speaking, coaching, and team-leading abilities, in addition to equipping you to offer training sessions. Telling stories has been the most effective form of communication since humans first invented language. For professional communicators, particularly corporate trainers and instructional designers, this is still true. In this book, I'll explain how to find, organise, and convey stories that will captivate audiences.

You just received a huge assignment. You may need to start a L&D department from scratch, receive a sizable learning project as a surprise, or have recently taken over an unsuccessful or even successful training department and are unsure of what to do. After you've taken a breath, you should first establish realistic expectations. There will be a lot of people in your business who have drastically different expectations for the learning department. You will almost certainly receive unsolicited advice about the construction process, the cost, and even how to provide instruction online. Your manager will demand something different from what your coworkers do.

How can you guarantee success?

In this book, I offer advice, guidelines, and suggestions that will assist you in establishing the right learning expectations with regard to the budget, gaining support, assessing training effectiveness, working with outside learning providers, and providing accurate time estimates for developing the learning. After completing this book, you will understand what expectations must be set and how to do so. I am delighted to share my knowledge, insights, and tried-and-true suggestions for establishing realistic learning objectives with you.

Why are some businesses so renowned?

It's their capacity for knowledge creation. Therefore, learning practitioners may apply quantifiable solutions for their businesses. I am specialised in bridging the gap between technical strategy and tactical objectives. And I assist in deconstructing complex technical ideas so you can apply them in your company to better yourself and the people around you. This book assists you in increasing learning and its effects by addressing essential measurement and assessment principles, as well as the many applications of these ideas through right business examples. You'll be in a position to challenge the current status quo for how learning is evaluated and enhanced, and you'll feel certain about the actions you can take to gain a deeper understanding of learning in your organisation.

A train the trainer concept increases a company's capability for training. This can save the cost of hiring outside trainers, speed up personnel upskilling, and ensure uniformity in training. Peer-to-peer learning is encouraged via the train the trainer programme. The organisation's culture and any potential obstacles the learner could run into while attempting to put the new knowledge into practise on the job are also understood by an internal SME turned trainer. Trainers will create a course with content that matters to the student in order to have the intended impact during a train the trainer programme. The first expert trainer, who now has a team of additional trainers, may utilise the freed-up time to work as a business consultant on other departments' requirements for departmental development, giving value to the entire organisation.

"The majority of articles and books about artificial intelligence focus on how people will be replaced by computers, taking away all of your jobs. The truth is less ominous, but technology will continue to alter the kinds of talents that organisations need to succeed."

To prepare your organisation for the future, it is essential to understand how things interact. The world is more chaotic and complicated than ever, but by enhancing intellect and giving people the tools they need to adapt and grow, learning technology has the ability to mitigate this complexity. The significance of comprehending how humans and artificial intelligence interact should be emphasised. Working together, humans and machines get the best outcomes. Due to the enormous volumes of data produced and its connection to people and how they engage with materials and technology, artificial intelligence and machine learning have a lot of potential for learning and development.

"The more effective an organisation's learning and development programmes are, the stronger and more profitable it becomes."

The strategic advantage of an organisation should be its talent. By investing the time to create a deliberate, strategic leadership development program, you can create the sort of leaders that advance the broader goals of your business. I will walk you through a multi-step procedure for creating and putting into action a high-impact leadership development programme that aids your firm in achieving its particular business goals. I will discuss how to carefully assess the demands of your business and use the results of that analysis to drive the design of your programme. The majority of aspects of life must now take sustainability into account, and L&D is no exception. As a result, you will examine how to develop a lasting learning culture in the future. L&D teams fall prey to short-term thinking much too frequently. It might be challenging to see beyond your current goals and make long-term plans in fast-paced situations. However, L&D must, however, adjust to a society where "sustainable" is a buzzword.

Organisational learning and development is a difficult endeavour that necessitates a diverse set of skills. Great learning and development professionals understand instructional design as well as the importance of creating learning cultures within organisations. They can also effectively convey the demands and objectives of learning to executives as well as workers. For seasoned instructional designers and corporate trainers who want to better grasp the function of learning in the workplace and how to successfully lead organisational learning, this learning path is the next logical step. I will demonstrate how to choose trainer, combine them with learning tools, and create materials that balance various forms of learning. I will also cover how to design a plan for success, make a budget, and manage your pilot project. An effective employee learning programme may serve as the foundation of a company rather than merely a means of employees training.

If done properly, it may help you manage upheaval, change, and transformation. However, it might be challenging to maintain morale. There are many other elements at play of which some are uncontrollable. The appropriate location and atmosphere are some of the most crucial aspects that frequently receive the least attention among those that you can influence. Don't forget to provide your staff with all the resources and assistance they might need to get the most out of the training course. Additionally, it entails preparing them mentally.

"A culture of learning can help us think differently while we are going through transformation. In order to address the continuously changing demands of customers, it is essential to promote large-scale experimentation to discover new solutions. Businesses must continuously experiment, measure, and learn if they are to keep up."
-Dr. Amit Das, Motivational Speaker, Mentor, Counsellor, and Coach.

Acknowledgements

*At the outset, I will thank my family for supporting me throughout the journey of writing my book and encouraging me to live my dreams; my son has always been instrumental in giving his inspiration to complete the writing of this book. Despite the fact that I am listed as the author of this book, **"Positive Psychology Of Learning And Development"** would not have been published if I had depended entirely on my own talents. Creating this book required more than anything—it took a family of dedicated and caring people who were always prepared to lend a hand.*

Writing a book while working full-time is no simple task, so I'd want to express my gratitude to my amazing coworkers who act as cheerleaders in equal measure. Thank you, too, to my students and clients for your patience and unflinching support while I worked on this book!

Thank you to everyone who has listened to me argue for doing everything you can to make your life, including your work life, more progressive. I appreciate everyone's assistance throughout the process. This book would not have been possible without each of you having had an impact on my life in some manner.

Lastly, I would like to thank all the people with whom I have been associated. You gave me power. I would like to thank Notion Press for publishing my book. Finally, thank you all for gifting your time to read this book.

I'd want to convey my heartfelt appreciation to the almighty God for bestowing his blessings and being so gracious.

CHAPTER ONE

A Positive Learning Culture Can Be A Growth Engine Of Organisational Transformation- Hope Or Reality

"An organisation's ability to learn, and translate that learning into action rapidly, is the ultimate competitive advantage." - Jack Welch

A prerequisite for organisational transformation is a culture of learning.

A corporate culture cannot be established by an organisation quickly, nor can it be altered. However, you can pinpoint the behaviours that are pertinent and crucial for fostering business agility, and you can then foster such behaviours within the framework of corporate culture across the board. Corporate culture can help or hinder a company's ability to adapt to change in relation to transformational initiatives to increase business agility. Corporate cultures that support systematic, ongoing learning for people, teams, and the entire business are said to have a "learning culture."

What does an organisation's learning culture entail?

I assure you that organisations that don't respect knowledge sharing have more serious problems. This is about individuals, not a millennial base, and the moment you begin developing your learning approach inside the framework of different generations, failure is certain. I object to the idea of "creating" a learning culture at this point. My belief is that it's more about nurturing than it is about constructing. Let's go through what culture is, shall we? Simply said, culture is about routine behaviours.

"Unconscious actions that are hard-wired into our brains and established in our surroundings are the things we naturally do. People who live in learning cultures instinctively seek out information as part of their workday, turn inward for self-discovery, and do research."

According to the learning organisation theory, culture is a set of fundamental presumptions that groups or organisations learn to use to solve issues with outward adaption and internal integration. This approach is recognised as legitimate and is taught to new employees of the company as a method to view conquering difficulties in the future. There are subsystems that must work together to transform a corporation into a learning organisation. They are the organisational structure, the workforce, the knowledge base, and technology.

"The only thing worse than training employees and losing them is to not train them and keep them."- Zig Ziglar

The biggest problems firms confront today include technological change; VUCCAD (Volatility, Uncertainty, Complexity, Conflict, Ambiguity, and Dynamism) circumstances exacerbated by the continuing epidemic; and altering organisational structures. Your job as a learning leader is to provide your team with the skills they need to be competitive in the face of these changes. In other words, you need to create an organisation that is prepared for change. It's not necessary to update your mission statement to reflect modern trends in order to be transformation-ready. Instead, the focus should be on creating a learning culture that will enable the entire business to adjust to the future's unavoidable unknowns.

The years 2020 and 2021 taught us how to adjust to quick changes in our working environment. It has forced us to learn how to use a variety of business-related digital platforms, like Stream Yard, Google Meet, Microsoft Teams, Zoom, and WebEx. Providing employees with chances for continuous learning, whether they work in an office, a hospital, their homes, or on a beach, will improve the organisation's return on investment (ROI) in 2022 and beyond. In addition to promoting employee morale, lowering attrition, and enhancing productivity, it also fosters innovation, which is necessary for growth and success.

"Businesses were negatively impacted by disruption, and the only organisations that were able to weather the volatility in the world economy were those that responded to the new changes."

If businesses invested the time to develop the necessary talents, their chances of success might rise. No matter their job title, function, or responsibilities, employees should be able to improve these abilities through learning programmes that are enabled by current technology in order to keep their teams nimble. Companies need to develop skills quickly, and they also want personnel with increasingly complicated skill profiles, including leadership qualities.

"By fostering an ongoing learning culture, organisations may develop the transformational mentality that must come before large undertakings."

Learning new knowledge and abilities puts your brain to the test, which might help you think more creatively. With time, effort, and the appropriate techniques, we must exercise the brain. The key is consistency over time, as organisations train staff for transformation like athletes may prepare for a marathon. Teams are inspired to think differently about the future and embrace innovation when learning is integrated early and frequently before and during a transformation journey.

According to research, almost 70% of transformational trips end in failure. This is due, in part, to the fact that transformational journeys, like any endeavour, need preparation. Organisational change might be compared to marathon training in that you wouldn't just turn up and expect to win. Teams must invest time and effort into acquiring the skills necessary to produce favourable results. Setting the stage for transformation initiatives is crucial to achieving objectives, whether they be better customer service, quicker value delivery, or more effective decision-making.

A culture of inquiry and learning serves as a driver for excellent performance, as evidenced by a survey in which 92% of workers said that curious people brought new ideas into teams and organisations. New ways of thinking bring new opportunities to the fore, as well as new talents and skills to realise those opportunities. Organisations should invest in developing a pre-transformation attitude before beginning any significant change to make the most of their efforts. This requires integration into every aspect of a company's operations and cannot be achieved by a single activity.

Learning may physically rewire your brains to promote innovation and help you break bad thought habits. In order to experience true change and generate innovative, customer-focused ideas, organisations need to adopt a discovery-focused, agile strategy that results from ongoing learning. According to research, there is a correlation between curiosity and creativity of 34% for every unit increase. People's curiosity may lead to workplace changes like increased creativity and open communication, both of which are crucial for transformation. Learning has the capacity to allow massive transformation by altering not just what you believe, your values and what you know, but also how you think and what you can achieve.

"A company has a learning culture when it places a high priority on helping its employees to comprehend its values, practises, beliefs, skill sets, and traditions."

Employees may then acquire the skills and information necessary to perform at their peak levels, better please clients, and contribute to the expansion of your business. In a recent analysis, which polled 832 talent development leaders, just 31% said that their company now has a "high" or "very high" level of a learning culture. The remaining respondents were divided between having a learning culture at a minor or moderate level, with only 6% of respondents reporting having no learning culture at all. These results demonstrate that creating a sustainable learning culture is an ongoing effort and that there is typically space for improvement, even if the majority of organisations understand its significance.

How may corporate cultural change be accelerated through learning?

Although it is a familiar saying, "culture eats strategy for breakfast," it is challenging to put into practise. Businesses are putting more emphasis on having the proper culture and mentality. An organisation's work culture has an impact on how it runs. It determines the organisation's output, financial success, and market viability. While each firm has its own set of ideals and procedures, they are all mainly influenced by the social mores, technical advancements, and commercial trends of the time in which they were founded. It's crucial to realise that these conventions vary with the passage of time.

Why is it vital to have a learning culture?

Learning cultures have an influence on every aspect of your organisation, from retention to production. In fact, according to IBM research on the importance of employee training, 84% of employees in the top-performing enterprises receive the training they require, compared to 16% in the bottom-performing businesses. Additionally, 94% of employees responded that investing in training and development is one of the main reasons they would want to remain in a position for a longer period of time. A critical component of success is having every team member understand and support the objectives of your company. Knowing your beliefs, product, consumers, mission, customs, organisation, and so on are important.

How can a developing company make sure every member is picking up the necessary knowledge?

A culture of learning is the solution. While creating a learning culture takes some time and work, the rewards are long-lasting and amazing. It matters to workers and aids in the expansion of your company, making it one of the most crucial organisational practises.

- Make learning a strategic thrust platform that supports the organisation's strategic success.
- Favor a "Show Your Work" atmosphere that makes work educational.
- Sharing knowledge inside a company should become routine.
- A company with a good learning culture accepts errors and even occasionally celebrates them.
- Leaders should deliberately enable mistakes to test firmly held beliefs in some instances, because mistakes are essential learning tools.

" You can't teach people everything they need to know. The best you can do is position them where they can find what they need to know when they need to know it."

- Make leadership a vital component of fostering learning.
- Leadership should be prepared to take responsibility for the entire learning culture and should not be restricted to HR or L&D.
- Employers may encourage workers to take personal responsibility for learning and to show their commitment to improvement by using onboarding programmes. Without giving employees the freedom to

speak out, decide for themselves, and take charge of their surroundings, businesses will not be able to learn.

"The culture of learning is focused on the improvement of human potential."

Learning cultures are inclusive of all participants, encourage experimentation, and encourage taking calculated risks. Interdependence, open and intense communication for teamwork, and information exchange are all encouraged in learning cultures. They also increase readiness and openness to learning from failures. Emotional commitment, organisational citizenship behaviour, and departure intention are all positively and significantly influenced by the learning culture of the organisation.

" Journeys are similar to learning experiences. The journey begins where learning is currently occuring and concludes when the learner has achieved greater accomplishment. Knowing more is not where the journey ends; action is. Without ongoing on-the-job training, employees cannot become more productive in every sense of the term."

The advantages of long-term learning for businesses organisations that foster a sustained learning culture benefit. With detailed analysis revealing that high-performing organisations are 5x more likely to have an extensive learning culture, top performers are also three times more likely to hold leaders accountable for communicating the value of learning, and they are twice as likely to indicate that their learning functions assist the organisation in achieving its business goals. Additionally, pre-hire interviews in top-performing learning cultures are 6x more likely to cover an employer's commitment to continued talent development. This data suggests that creating a sustainable learning culture has several advantages. It goes without saying that knowledge is a worthwhile endeavour and that learning is a prize in and of itself. However, from a business-focused viewpoint, organisations with enduring learning cultures frequently outperform their rivals.

How would you get executive buy-in for your learning initiatives?

It might take time and effort to get support for a learning programme. And when you secure buy-in for starting the programme, you may also need to secure buy-ins for future growth and expansion. Let's begin by getting people to buy in first.

1. Determine how the learning and development activities you are proposing will support the organisational strategic or operational goals.
2. Leaders like to hear about improvements in the productivity of their individual employees rather than the inherent benefit of learning or how it improves and makes people better in general. or a rise in sales. They desire improvements to the key performance metrics within their control.
3. You've made a significant step toward buy-in if you can demonstrate how your learning and development initiatives can boost the revenue of their department or division.
4. The department heads need to hear from you on how learning and development might help with their particular issues.
5. Executives need to hear how learning and development support their pursuit of their objectives.

6. By conducting one-on-one talks and creating a slide presentation that makes a strong case for why L&D activities are beneficial, you aim to gradually gain support.

7. It won't be simple since learning and development initiatives are frequently viewed as an expense rather than an investment. The debate has to be reframed with an investment focus rather than a cost focus.

8. Every organisations will have different learning requirements, but the leadership gap is frequently a common factor. In order to fill this gap, leadership development programmes are in great demand, and research demonstrates that they are effective—these programmes have been found to boost team engagement, enhance retention, and lower the cost of hiring outside. For such initiatives, establish clear objectives and regularly assess their success.

9. Plan on-going measures to assess their effects, such as using qualitative staff survey feedback, and be ready to share updates on target progress at all times.

10. Employing managers should search for candidates that exhibit traits like insight and a growth mindset. Senior managers should set aside time for training for their immediate reports.

11. The executive leadership should take on the role of L&D's strongest supporters and evangelise for preserving the learning culture.

12. The days when possessing absolute authority meant you were a leader are long gone. Today's leaders must be able to inspire others and persuade them to follow their example so that they may work together to create something bigger. This is what Bersin refers to as "followership."

13. By cultivating a following of learners, L&D executives can empower their organisations to adapt to a business environment that is changing before our eyes.

14. Client happiness is the key to a successful business, yet in the modern world, customer needs are always shifting. Businesses must thus adapt quickly to these changes.

15. There's no denying that in recent years, demand for agile management approaches has increased significantly. Agile learning is an incremental and iterative method of organisational management. It supports teams in keeping up with the requirements of the contemporary workplace while concentrating on the prompt delivery of commercial value.

16. Last but not least, you need to incorporate a strategy for gauging the success of your learning and development initiatives.

17. Obtain important information regarding your efforts. I've discovered that while you don't need to measure all of your learning and development efforts, you do need to choose one or two important programmes and demonstrate how they directly affect the bottom line or support important strategic drivers, and then widely distribute that data within the organisation. But, regrettably, there is no assurance that support will last indefinitely even if you use these three strategies to get early buy-in.

18. You must regularly engage with leaders to reiterate the importance of learning and development initiatives if you want to maintain support.

19. By developing a governance framework where leadership from both groups shares responsibility for conceiving, prioritising, planning, and procuring

funding for capability-building initiatives, L&D departments may strengthen their collaboration with business executives.

20. The chief experience officer (CXO), senior executives, and business-unit leaders of a firm will create the people-capability agenda for various enterprise segments and make sure that it is in line with the company's overall strategy under this governance model.

21. The learning function and all L&D efforts will be thoroughly ingrained in the organisational culture with the assistance of top business leaders. Senior leadership's engagement ensures complete commitment to the longer-term goal of the L&D department.

22. Create a strategy right away to communicate information and the outcomes of your work that shows what L&D has accomplished over time.

23. Work to participate in the early planning stages of new business initiatives and consistently showcase advancements, safety records, and other outcomes that have a direct bearing on L&D.

24. Keep in mind that in order for an L&D initiative to succeed, buy-in must be obtained and maintained. If you employ these strategies, you'll be on the right track to gaining and keeping the support required to run a successful L&D company.

25. A hybrid approach to learning is necessary for cultivating this discovery attitude; in my experience, learning is most effective when individuals can choose the learning style that works best for them and immediately apply principles to their jobs.

26. A work-based learning programme that enables individuals to adapt and truly adopt the abilities needed

to take on novel and developing initiatives should be taken into consideration.

27. Make sure staff members have the opportunity to observe the outcomes of their learning, as this can encourage further involvement.

How can L&D effectively contribute to business growth?

To be effective, L&D must carefully assess employee competencies and decide which ones are most crucial to assisting in the implementation of the business plan for the organisation. To make sure they are developing a people-capability agenda that actually represents business priorities and strategic objectives, L&D executives should periodically review this alignment. Companies need to become more flexible and prepared to adjust their business practises and procedures as new tools and technology are continually being developed. Similarly, L&D divisions must be ready to quickly begin capability-building initiatives, for instance, if unexpected business demands materialise or personnel suddenly need instruction in cutting-edge technologies like cloud-based collaboration tools.

"It is particularly difficult in the digital age of today when social and cultural influence comes from many different sources, many of which fall beyond the boundaries of corporate control or influence paradigms. It is no secret that flexible hours, remote work, gig-based employment, and 24x7 digital connectivity are quickly replacing traditional 9 to 5 workdays."

Organisations may make sure that the upcoming workforce has the skills and knowledge necessary to thrive by setting up a mentoring programme that pairs more experienced workers with less experienced colleagues. The saying "you can't teach an old dog new tricks" is absolutely untrue when it comes to L&D. Actually, more seasoned workers have a lot to contribute in terms of expertise and knowledge, and it's simpler than you may imagine to train them to guide your younger workers. It is important to recognise the importance more seasoned workers bring to the table in terms of learning and growth. Their participation in learning and development can help bridge the generational divide.

"Organisations may progress toward learning and long-lasting transformation through integrating people and structures via learning strategy."

Values, precepts, and assumptions that support the achievement of collective learning across the board of a company are referred to as the learning culture. Learning culture from organisational culture differs or is unique in comparison to other organisational cultures such as labour culture, service culture, or mutual culture. The company's main value is learning, thanks to its learning culture.

Today's effective L&D department needs to distribute itself horizontally across its company in smart and deliberate ways in order to escape its vertical silo. The areas that L&D leaders should give priority to in the upcoming time are given below.

- Ask your colleagues for assistance. Most L&D executives claim that while cross-functional collaboration has improved over the last year, there is still an opportunity for improvement.
- As skills-based recruiting becomes more significant, there is an opportunity to partner with talent acquisition, and L&D executives should work more closely with people analytics to better assess the effects of their initiative.

- Cross-functional collaborations within L&D have increased year over year. Keep in touch with your stakeholders. Compared to pre-pandemic periods, L&D leaders are now twice as likely to claim a place at the C-suite table.
- In the future, keeping this seat will require tying learning initiatives to business effects based on important corporate goals, such as internal mobility.
- Learning professionals should think about outsourcing more clerical and administrative work to free up time to focus on the things that really matter to their business.
- L&D is well-positioned to become a connector of people, resources, and experiences that provide employees with ongoing growth and success. Previously, L&D served as the curators, designers, and implementers of learning content and curriculum.
- From onboarding to professional development to departure, L&D will integrate company needs with employee needs, creating pertinent opportunities for people to challenge themselves every day throughout their entire career.
- To guarantee that you are eventually supporting a performance life cycle that meets workers' ambitions, from talent acquisition and onboarding to overall enhanced engagement and flourishing within an inclusive culture, you are collaborating with other HR functions.
- Nearly half of L&D professionals anticipate an increase in their spending this year. Given the amount of work L&D is expected to accomplish, this is fantastic news. Leaders in L&D now need to spend the funding wisely.
- Investing in connections, political capital, resources, and oneself is how L&D professionals succeed.

- Many L&D professionals have kept their performance metrics the same, despite the fact that learning programmes are becoming more strategic and cross-functional.
- In 2022, qualitative feedback will continue to be the primary method through which learning leaders will assess the effectiveness of their upskilling and reskilling initiatives, which have the potential to have a significant positive impact. By tying skills to internal mobility and staff retention, leaders may increase their effect.
- Microlearning in little doses spread out throughout the course of a worker's week can have a significant influence. To help with this, L&D teams may creatively make use of already-existing resources.
- One example is dedicating a channel on the business's digital communication platform to sharing daily observations. Employees who have a few minutes to spare can be reached via weekly emails that offer fresh learning materials.
- Learning and development (L&D) has a new responsibility to become its best self in this period of profound transition. L&D executives are responding to the workers' renewed requests for development and meaning while also juggling the pressing issue of future-proofing their companies.
- Learning leaders are breaking through conventional silos as a result of L&D's change in order to work together on a more comprehensive vision for HR.
- Your leaders are the first step in establishing a learning culture inside your organisation. After all, if leaders don't follow their own advice, why would employees take sustainable learning seriously?

- Modern learning management systems (LMS) and employee training software platforms make it much simpler for L&D professionals to automatically create different types of new training and development content from a single core training piece, saving them time from having to manually repurpose it into different content formats.
- L&D specialists are more highly appreciated than ever before across enterprise firms as a result of successfully adjusting to the new "Zoom" era of work.
- Teams with established learning cultures have a greater chance of attracting top talent, as evidenced by the fact that such organisations are three times more likely to use their learning culture in the recruiting process.
- The organisation's learning strategy and different services are created or supported by these organisations, it is obvious that they (HR or OD teams) are actively participating in fostering a healthy culture of learning.
- Repurposing current training materials into multimodal learning materials or reformatting the same L&D course materials across video, audio, text, and visual content is a trend to watch in 2022.
- Everything boils down to mindset once more. Adopting a growth mindset for L&D teams opens up a world of opportunities, including anchoring a sustainable learning culture, as I recently addressed in my piece on fixed vs. growth mindsets.
- I observed that managers frequently allot time for giving feedback to workers but not for them to focus on their areas for development. If managers want to see their employees' progress, they must provide time for learning. Additionally, learning time should be shielded

from the numerous other responsibilities that intrude on it.

- Constructive criticism is an effective approach for assisting workers in developing crucial abilities in areas where they may be lacking. This external input is essential for progress because it might be challenging for us to see our own limitations.
- Set a good example. Senior management is looked upon by employees for leadership and guidance. You must engage in your own learning if you want your staff to do the same.
- Be certain that everyone on your team sees learning as an essential part of their job. In a fast-paced, digital environment, learning helps employees maintain a broad perspective and stay current.
- Managers must demonstrate that learning is an essential component of the job in order for it to become an active element of the workplace. This book recommends that management sets a strong example for chances for learning and personal growth.
- Celebrate development and consider mistakes. To advance as team members and people, they must be able to acknowledge their accomplishments and draw lessons from them.
- Encourage employee participation by providing engaging programming and opportunities.
- Encourage new experiences and make sure that what is learned is useful in the workplace. Both staff members and senior management need to have the same goals when it comes to personal growth and development.
- The bulk of learning in today's businesses is not just unproductive; its goal, timing, and substance are also incorrect.

What is the crital role of HR in optimising an organisation's learning culture?

One department or programme can not possess or build a healthy culture of learning. It is sustained by the combined efforts of all community members. With all the newest bells and whistles that technology has to offer, you may have an astounding selection of learning options.

However, you cannot have a healthy culture of learning if individuals believe it is unsafe to take risks and make errors. I want you to concentrate on four tasks that talent pros must complete that are vitally necessary. You must first concentrate on the two components of the learning environment. How you encourage personal development and growth, as well as how you foster an atmosphere where taking chances and making errors are acceptable.

You won't be successful if you don't focus on both halves. Soil contaminated by sunlight alone cannot be cleaned up. This implies that you must continuously monitor important KPIs. Attrition of your finest employees, psychological safety, improvements and advancement, and employee engagement. And you need to take proactive action until things change when you spot a team or region that isn't flourishing. The whole enterprise is undercut if you don't.

Corporate learning initiatives from L&D should be a priority on the HR agenda, just as they should be for the company. L&D is crucial to the workforce, succession planning, performance management, onboarding, and promotion processes. Our study reveals that many L&D activities, at best, have only hazy ties to yearly performance assessments and don't have a defined strategy or follow-up to performance-management procedures.

In order for people to quickly contribute to the team effort, you must also incorporate the essential elements of learning culture within your learning offerings. For instance, your management and leadership training must show executives how to foster a development mindset, provide psychological safety, deliver successful coaching, offer and accept helpful criticism, and exhibit emotional intelligence, such as empathy. These components, as well as instructions on how to empower their own growth both through their supervisor or team and, if necessary, by surrounding them, are required for employee programmes. By exposing them to the principles of continuous improvement and the tools and support that are available to them, your onboarding process should make it simple for new hires to fit in with a productive learning environment.

Workplace ethical culture, which is mediated by perceived ethical leadership, greatly improves all aspects of job engagement—vigor, devotion, and absorption. Additionally, the learning culture significantly and favourably affects the employees' capacity for learning. Employees will be consistently encouraged by learning cultures to engage in learning activities on an individual, group, and organisational level during their daily routine activities.

The effectiveness and impact of a learning approach should be assessed using key performance indicators (KPIs). The first indication evaluates the degree to which all L&D investments and efforts are in line with business goals. The second KPI examines whether learning interventions alter people's performance and behaviour. Last but not least, an operational-excellence KPI gauges the efficiency of resources and investments made in corporate academies.

Since accurate assessment is rarely straightforward, many businesses continue to use outdated performance indicators like satisfaction and completion rates for learning programmes. However, high-performing firms put more emphasis on outcomes-based indicators, including the influence on employee engagement, teamwork, and business process improvement.

> *"The goal of an organisational learning culture is to support and enable workers' participation in both individual and group learning activities that will benefit the growth, performance, and success of the business."*

Work involvement also includes the intention to leave and the affective commitment. In the long term, it will increase and improve learning agility. Learning ability and learning agility are two separate things. The capacity of an individual to adapt quickly and nimbly to new and challenging conditions is known as learning agility.

You must model a perfect learning culture and provide a real example for others to follow. It's accurate to say that HR, L&D are the culture's custodians. Always, the organisation demonstrates how well-rounded and talented the professional teams are. I've observed this in every organisation I've ever worked with. The rest of the organisation is hampered when HR and L&D are not prospering, and I'm not the only one who notices this. For your needs, the HR and L&D teams must be environments where taking chances and making errors are acceptable. People must often participate in learning, and managers must excel in coaching. It is exceedingly challenging to establish a positive learning culture across the business if these teams don't lead by example.

At least 30% of your evaluation should include information on your efforts to grow and learn. You must take this into consideration when deciding how to bestow benefits like increases and bonuses. This part is called "walk the talk." The importance of learning must be demonstrated consistently and openly, such as via evaluations and awards, if you actually want to foster a culture that encourages it. Once your evaluation is finished, use it to create an action plan so that you can start fixing problems and enhancing your company right away.

Finally, a strong learning culture must be supported by your systems and procedures. This is particularly relevant to your performance management system. You are missing something extremely important if you solely evaluate performance in terms of results. You must measure and appreciate progress and improvement in order to build a growth mindset.

***Do you do reality checking on the growing importance
of sustainable learning culture in an organisation?***

The Association for Talent Development (ATD), offers intriguing insight into the fundamental components of a learning culture. According to the report, a learning culture must have synergy between corporate strategy and ongoing professional development. Other noteworthy traits include having a professional staff with the necessary qualifications to manage the learning function; allocating funds specifically for meeting the organisation's learning needs; and incorporating talented, nurturing learning leaders into the overall talent management processes. The evidence backs up our first suspicions.

***"A business must have organisational missions, visions,
and values that support and align with the demands of
employee growth if it is to have a strong learning culture."***

Although offering learning opportunities is an important part of creating and sustaining a culture of learning, there are other factors to consider. A great leader will motivate their staff to prioritise learning in their personal growth plan.

Because learning has a beneficial influence on strategy, creativity, employee engagement, staff retention, and many other areas, a learning culture is a crucial component of long-term organisational success. Team members have the time and space to continuously expand their knowledge and gain new skills in organisations with learning cultures. The learning is designed to assist and enhance employee progress on both a personal and professional level.

- *Why learning culture is so crucial for long-term success?*
- *How it helps individuals and their businesses?*
- *How it encourages creativity?*
- *What is a culture of continuous learning?*

By encouraging professional growth and fostering a culture of lifelong learning, employees may acquire new information and abilities that will help them flourish in their work. Employee happiness, commitment, and engagement increase when personal growth opportunities are encouraged and supported.

As a leader, you can guarantee that there is a deeper alignment of culture and values with workers, strengthening the business and putting it in a position for long-term success. Due to the close connection between learning and an organisation's success, leaders who adopt a learning-focused approach to overall management will integrate learning into the organisation's mission and business strategy by offering a variety of opportunities to meet employees' needs for personal growth and development.

Employees must feel as though they are making progress in terms of their intellectual and skill development. When individuals receive assistance in choosing and achieving their learning objectives, they experience more happiness in both their professional and personal lives. This also improves client satisfaction.

In addition to helping executives develop their organisations and create high-performing teams by ensuring that people achieve their professional and personal objectives, learning cultures also benefit customers. Employees are more committed to the company and better equipped to serve their clients when they have an improved attitude and work for a leadership group that fosters inquiry and innovation at all levels.

Making a learning plan based on the organisation's business and talent strategies is one of an L&D executive's main responsibilities. The learning plan aims to enhance professional growth and increase company-wide competencies on schedule and at a reasonable cost. Additionally, the learning method helps strengthen corporate culture and motivates staff to uphold the company's core principles.

"A learning culture is one that encourages curiosity, a thirst for information, and group learning that is pertinent to the objectives and mission of the company."

Although most businesses and organisations are far from these values, it is nevertheless feasible to put them into practise. Employee learning opportunities and personal development are frequently linked to increasing employee engagement and feedback. To establish your unique learning culture, think about implementing these suggestions:Create a systematic system of rewards for long-term, ongoing learning. Long-term requirements include fostering critical thinking and encouraging employee involvement in novel concepts and knowledge acquisition.

Over the past few decades, the nature of employment has changed from lifelong employment to one in which employees are maintained only as long as they can offer value to an organisation. People place "opportunities for learning and development" as the top criterion because employees are now responsible for their own professional and personal progress. On the other hand, one of the main justifications for quitting a firm is a lack of L&D.

"Learning-focused organisations are more competitive in their markets because they take less risk."

This advantage extends to performance, hiring and retention, employee engagement, customer service, succession planning, and innovation. Here are just a few incredible things that a learning culture may accomplish for a company: Improve performance growing up in a learning culture allows team members to adopt improved attitudes and actively seek out chances to learn and share information with their teams, both of which have a beneficial effect on an organisation's overall well-being and potential for future success.

"Strong learning cultures promote adaptability, flexibility, and innovation in organisations. Additionally, they are less inclined to be risk-averse and more likely to welcome change, draw in, and keep top talent."

Multiple research data analysis indicate that firms with a robust network of high-performing individuals are more likely to have a complete learning culture than firms with people that perform at a lower level. Significantly, great performers are more likely to attribute their success in meeting organisational business goals to an extensive learning culture.

According to research compiled by LinkedIn, employees who spend time learning on the job are 47% less likely to be stressed, 39% more likely to feel successful and productive, 23% more capable of taking on additional responsibilities, and 21% more likely to feel confident and content. These numbers show that organisations that prioritise learning have substantially higher rates of employee engagement. For this reason, making a culture of learning a part of your organisation's goal is crucial.

"Learning cultures are a magnet for drawing highly competent people searching for companies that offer chances for professional growth when it comes to recruiting and retention."

Any organisation's culture of caring should include a commitment to employee growth and development. One of the finest and most impactful ways a leader can show a culture of caring and uphold company values is by fostering a learning environment.

"Organisations with excellent learning cultures may draw top talent, engage and keep people, and improve performance and employee happiness, as I've highlighted."

Strong leadership abilities call for a significant amount of training and mentoring. Organisational learning may foster commitment, employee buy-in, and the development of institutional DNA, all of which can assist leaders in creating effective succession planning. Retirements and other changes will take place as businesses develop and evolve through time, leaving vacancies in high management roles. The organisation's future success depends on finding the ideal team members to fill these jobs. To facilitate smooth transitions, a pool of competent applicants who are knowledgeable about leadership concepts should be developed.

"A good leader will be well-read on a wide range of subjects and dedicated to maintaining a culture that encourages staff to grow continuously."

A culture of learning is crucial to creating future leaders in your business and creating a solid succession plan. If your company already fosters a culture of learning, you are well aware of the advantages this has for your business. However, you should also be conscious of the potential for success a learning culture will offer, as well as the future leadership requirements of your company.

How will you create a competitive edge with your unparalleled learning culture?

A competitive advantage basically entails outperforming rivals in terms of quality, speed, or effectiveness. So how can learning provide you with a competitive edge? There are multiple ways that giving learning value might improve your business.

1. Organisation respond more rapidly than rivals to factors like market developments, consumer requests, and even actual occurrences when learning is ingrained in the corporate culture.

2. You learn one day that your rival had developed an online compliance course for a new rule and that it would be made available at the end of the week. What then did you do? You worked all night in order to create your own online course on the same legislation.

3. You made it available a day ahead of your rivals. Why is this example relevant, then? Without a talented, educated, and properly trained crew, this organisation would never have been able to do this. The business was able to change because it valued education.

4. Organisations that consider learning as a competitive advantage can move more quickly than those that are not learning-focused. Adaptability comes in second.

5. CEOs, managers, and even front-line managers frequently lament that staff members dislike change. But adaptability must be woven into the very fabric of an organisation.

6. Change should not be viewed as a barrier but rather as a fresh learning challenge that must be overcome. It turns out that being open to change and adaptability is a byproduct of learning concentration. But it also indicates that learning happens in the workplace.

7. Employees learn from one another when mistakes are made. Therefore, companies that consider learning as a competitive advantage are more adaptable and fluid than those that do not.

8. Develop your employer brand. One of a company's most valuable assets is its brand, which communicates a lot about its market performance, financial stability, position in the market, and range of goods and services.

9. Investments in L&D may improve a company's reputation as an "employer of choice" and strengthen its brand. Employers must put forth more effort to compete for a limited pool of talent as significant portions of the workforce prepare to retire. They must use an employer value proposition to expressly communicate their brand strength in order to do this.

10. The pairing of two or more items that don't seem to go together creatively. And it serves as the gasoline for the contemporary corporate ecology.

11. Employees who are learning new processes are better equipped to put those seemingly unrelated concepts together. Because learning provides them with

perspective, they can develop those new items and find solutions to issues.

12. You are encouraged to maintain your problem-solving approach in a learning setting in addition to being given the tools to be creative. Employees won't have much possibility for creativity if they aren't given the chance to research or think about various topics.

13. Employees that are given opportunities for growth and training tend to share more inside their organisations. Compared to organisations where knowledge is kept to themselves, they are more receptive to discussing ideas. It challenges the idea that only select individuals should have access to particular information.

14. Different types of sharing can take place, and by creating formal sharing scenarios like training, you can also create informal learning opportunities.

"The culture of learning expands across the organisation through informal and formal information exchange."

To maintain its value, human capital needs continuing investments in L&D. The value of human capital falls when knowledge ages or is forgotten—a phenomenon that occurs more quickly today—and must be replenished by new learning and useful job experience. Investments in the next generation of leaders are paying off handsomely for businesses. According to research, businesses with the best leadership beat other businesses in terms of earnings before interest, taxes, depreciation, and amortisation by almost two times (EBITDA).

Additionally, businesses that invest in developing leaders through major changes have a 2.4-times higher chance of exceeding their performance goals. When the workforce is becoming more virtual and distributed throughout the globe, L&D may support the development of a values-based culture and a feeling of community in organisations. Millennials, in particular, are enthusiastic about working with ethical, environmentally friendly companies that advance societal wellbeing.

Although it is the most evident benefit, it also has the most influence. Training expansion results in knowledge expansion and performance expansion. For me, learning new information from a fantastic training session increases my passion, energises me, and improves my ability to perform my work. That feels wonderful. Imagine that mentality empowering your whole enterprise. Speed, flexibility, creativity, organisational sharing, and enhanced knowledge and performance are those benefits that come from using learning to gain a competitive edge.

"It starts at the top, and it starts with having a CEO or a senior leader that truly values learning and talks about it very aggressively."- Matthew Smith, CLO at McKinsey & Company.

The cultural principles that have contributed to the company's success will be ingrained in ideal applicants. Having "cultural continuity" is crucial during transitional periods, and a culture of learning may make changes easier. Your company has prepared the way for exceptional people to fill future leadership roles by including mentorship and leadership training in your learning culture.

A learning culture is one in which making mistakes while attempting new things is actively encouraged. Innovation really shines when there is a culture that supports making errors and learning things that go above and beyond a person's specific job responsibilities.

A culture where innovation is the norm and all team members are invested in it as a daily, participatory practise may be developed in your business by intentionally establishing a culture of curiosity and encouraging individual learning.

A learning mentality is fostered by expanding one's knowledge base outside of the field directly related to one's professional function. Additionally, it enables workers to make connections in a way that is not possible for workers who do not benefit from a learning culture. Employees' knowledge can be expanded beyond the responsibilities of their regular jobs in learning cultures. Learning cultures build teams that welcome and thrive on creativity and risk-taking more through promoting learning mindsets. I will share some intriguing perspectives on the relationship between learning cultures and creativity in this chapter.

"When discussing the significance of deliberate training, I believe that training on hard skills and the compliance requirements that businesses are often compelled to offer account for around 60% of the learning that occurs on the job when discussing the significance of training."

You are all aware of the mandatory compliance training and hard skill requirements that must be completed on the job. These requirements are an important part of on-the-job training, but they sometimes seem more like checks off a list than meaningful learning. The remaining 40% of learning, which is more flexible and "elective," is what businesses encourage but do not demand in order to comply with regulatory requirements.

Your team will be exposed to "big picture" concepts, which are crucial for innovation, during this form of learning. It can encourage innovative thinking across departments when you provide employees with these opportunities as part of a culture of personal growth and professional development beyond compliance. According to a Deloitte survey, high-performing learning firms are 92% more likely to innovate. Furthermore, 46% prefer to be the first to market.

Learning is a business strategy that will expand your company, offer it a competitive edge, and support it through any changes that could occur. Additionally, it will provide your team with the resources they need to succeed. How to instil a culture of learning at work By fostering a learning culture, L& D executives can empower their businesses to adapt to a business environment that is changing before our very eyes.

Companies are also using online learning, social networking, and even incentives to provide staff with the necessary skill sets. Companies may advance in the face of continual change by ensuring that their personnel have the necessary skills. Thus, implementing tactics for continuous learning helps to foster a culture where learning is highly valued and progress is the only accepted standard.

Companies are undertaking a number of learning and development programmes with the goal of encouraging a culture of continual learning at work. Many businesses are collaborating with thorough learning management systems that use technology to find and close skills gaps in the workforce. These systems not only identify skills gaps but also forecast the skill sets that will be needed in the future to support the organisation's growth using technologies like artificial intelligence and machine learning.

What are the defining characteristics of cultural organisation?

A company must promote a learning culture in order to equip workers for transformation. Employees that work in such a culture acquire the mental habits that enable them to identify outmoded procedures and promptly and effectively implement essential adjustments. Ask yourself if the atmosphere you're fostering exhibits the following traits to see if your company is developing toward a learning culture.

Does the workplace environment foster and reward sage employees?

There is no assurance that information gained now will address issues in the future or that skills will always be in demand. But perceptive staff members can spot when a problem's nature changes. They then apply their understanding to sharpen their abilities and look for new information. These qualities enable employees to take on fresh challenges, which enables the entire business to change.

However, insight is not a natural talent. It must be fostered by culture by giving workers the chance to learn, investigate exciting concepts, and try out novel solutions. Additionally, they must support the goal of lifelong learning. Is it laudatory of development mindsets?

Robert Keagan, a psychologist and professional development consultant, discovered via his research that individuals in the majority of organisations make a significant effort to cover up their flaws and unmet learning requirements. It takes so much work that Keagan views it as a second job. Such role-playing has detrimental effects on both the company and its employees. It takes time and effort from workers that could be used toward genuine progress. Organisations continue to pay for these fruitless initiatives. Keagan suggests that a learning culture encourages growth mindsets because of these above mentioned factors.

"Learning is not viewed as a sign of weakness but rather of character in this sort of organisation. Failure is not the opposite of success; rather, it is a necessary component of progress. Even the most intelligent employee cannot handle every task. Sometimes it will take too much time to perfect a new talent."

Perceptive employees must make connections with others whose complementing abilities might be useful. The assistance they require is compartmentalised in a different department. And it can be a challenging obstacle to overcome inside the hyper-specialised architecture of many modern enterprises. On the other hand, companies with a learning culture strive to remove these obstacles. They achieve this by establishing cross-departmental learning opportunities, peer-to-peer information exchange platforms, and mentorships for interdepartmental skill-sharing.

To comprehend patterns and present L&D goals, I conducted many rounds of studies "From evolution to revolution". Through my work, I am able to demonstrate how the L&D function is evolving to suit the companies' shifting demands as well as the rising levels of investment in professional development. L&D executives must accept a bigger position within the business and create an ambitious vision for the function in order to maximise investments in training initiatives and curriculum development. A thorough, coordinated approach that involves the organisation and promotes teamwork is a crucial element of this effort.

Are the organisation's leaders cultivating it?

It is obvious that in the commercial world of today, transition is the norm. The day will eventually come when tried-and-true methods will stop working. Reactionary groups fear and crumble when this occurs. However, businesses that are prepared for change adapt, and this process starts with the employees. When they work in an environment that values learning, employees may develop the resilience and agility they need to adjust to shifting market conditions and expectations.

Everyone in an organisation is greatly impacted by the actions of the leaders. Directors who want their managers to develop must set a good example by being open to learning themselves. For managers who want to see their team members advance, the same is true.

"Leadership culture must change from a group of "know-it-alls" to one of "learn-it-alls."

Learn-it-alls give you licence to confess your shortcomings and desire for improvement. From a group of "know-it-alls" to a group of "learn-it-alls," leadership must change. This necessitates cultivating intellectually humble leaders that are always willing to learn, dedicated to growth, and never use their knowledge or position to demoralise others. It will take intellectual humility for you to model such abilities and open, honest dialogue with influential leaders.

How should a learning leader proceed?

Building a learning culture takes time. Employers must make a conscious effort to improve their workforce, which necessitates smart investment decisions. The following things should be taken into account when you start to create a learning culture at your company:

- Budget when budget cuts are necessary, education is frequently the first to suffer. Decisions like these unfortunately result in piecemeal efforts that aren't conducive to continuous learning. They also send a negative message about the value education holds throughout the entire organisation.
- One way to maintain a consistent budget is to gain buy-in by making the value of learning explicitly clear.
- Write a mission statement that aligns your vision with organisational objectives, then choose and design programmes with ROI in mind.
- Learning cultures are crucial for fostering the innovative, nuanced thinking that makes businesses successful and maintains them that way by assisting them in being flexible and adaptive when markets and other circumstances change.
- Strong learning cultures meet employees' fundamental needs for development and mastery while also demonstrating to prospective employees that an employer is willing to invest in their long-term growth and development.
- Innovative business owners will include their organisation's learning culture into the hiring procedure to attract top talent.
- Potential workers should be able to see during the hiring process that the business is committed to a culture of learning and continuous growth and would really support staff members who pursue professional development opportunities.
- Candidates who are seeking chances for intellectual and professional advancement will respond favourably to employers who declare their commitment to a culture of talent development throughout the interview process.

- Creating and improving a plan requires constant learning. In order to find new markets, find the best consumers to serve in those markets, and find the best ways to service those customers, managers and staff that value learning are better able to do so.
- Making continuous learning a top priority in your company is not only a wise move, but it's also essential in a world that is always changing.
- The importance of giving staff these special learning chances to advance and evolve is tremendous, whether it be through on-site training, online courses, or just revisiting existing procedures and previous errors to support a continuous improvement attitude.
- Recall that any company with a "zero tolerance" policy for errors would only succeed in cultivating an environment where people don't feel appreciated and are so afraid of failing that creativity cannot flourish.
- Leaders who have the insight to see that errors can frequently be transformed into opportunities and who work in an environment where learning is valued highly are more likely to achieve tremendous success.
- The lives of their employees will be significantly improved as a result, which will make the process of increasing innovation, customer service, retention, and engagement much simpler and more natural.
- No matter how efficient a learning programme claims to be, it won't help if employees lack the time to take part. Google and other companies have implemented the 80/20 rule because of this. Employees may spend 20% of their time learning, growing, and experimenting with new concepts.
- Although this ratio can change, having a written guideline helps to emphasise how important learning is.

- Leadership in L&D must be familiar with key HR management procedures and work closely with HR executives.
- The most effective L&D departments use performance reviews' collected development feedback as a starting point for their capability-building agenda.
- Annual performance reviews are increasingly being replaced by regular, real-time feedback in businesses.
- The L&D role can aid managers in developing the abilities necessary to give development feedback in this regard.

"I've talked to companies that have rationed learning to the degree that if you're not rated high in the performance management process, you don't get to go to learning" -Josh Bersin, The founder of Bersin by Deloitte.

Business organisations go through disruptive changes that are both ongoing and episodic. These modifications necessitate transformational efforts in addition to transitional and developmental ones for the company. Organisational culture was one of those elements that caused business transformations in several well-known organisations to fail.

Organisational culture is strategically important in managing and transforming businesses. For companies, change could serve as an advantage or a burden. The evolution of corporate culture should have an effect on employees' capacity for learning as well as their level of engagement at work.

Organisational culture can be distinguished from learning culture and hierarchal-centralistic culture based on impact. Learning culture is mapped and reflected into multiple dimensions using the concept of a "culture map":

communicating, evaluating, persuading, leading, deciding, trusting, disagreeing, and scheduling. Management practitioners have a road map for creating a learning culture thanks to their mapping of the current situation's cultural gap.

Why does organisational transformation fail?

The change in the workforce may be fueled by a new generation of robots and machine learning. But there is little doubt that corporate learning culture will play a role in how effective the transition is. When confronting a change problem, businesses all too frequently fail to consider cultural challenges. The things that will eventually revolutionise how and what we do in the workplace—digital technology, artificial intelligence, and applications of machine learning—almost always receive the greatest attention.

What about a company's ability to accept transformative change, though? Are leaders ready to accept the transformational message? Do workers possess the flexibility and mentality necessary to commit to a completely different way of working? According to a recent poll, the most frequent external causes of workforce change have been identified. Surprisingly, 70% of respondents stated that advancements in digital technologies are driving the need to reimagine workforces. When I inquired about the factors that hinder a successful change, the conversation went from machinery to culture.

In fact, learning culture was named as the single largest obstacle to a successful change by 54% of respondents. I need to take a close look at what we mean by "culture" in order to fully understand that statistic and why it could be the most important insight into transformational projects. The beliefs, actions, and attitudes of learning of workers from all parts of the company and at all levels of hierarchy make up an organisation's learning culture. How learning assignments are completed, goals are set, and interpersonal relationships are exhibited through an organisation's learning culture.

Today's employees frequently indicate their continuing professional education (CPE) credits in order to strengthen their case for promotion. Instead of concentrating on the effect they have on the business, L&D workers also demonstrate their value by achieving faulty KPIs, such as the total number of CPE credits employees obtain. The latter is simpler to assess yet also produces erroneous outputs, such as the following: The timing of your learning is incorrect. When learning is required, people learn best.

One's attention and desire to study are strengthened when they are put to use in practical settings. Although psychologist Edwin Locke demonstrated the benefits of brief feedback loops in 1968 with his theory of motivation, it is still not a common practise in business training. As a result, employees of today frequently study the same material on L&D's timetable at a time when it has no immediate application to their job, and as a result, their learning suffers.

Businesses must confirm that their staff can carry out their business goals after identifying them—a job that may be trickier than it seems. Some businesses put little or no effort into evaluating employees' talents, while others only do so at a high level. Speaking with L&D, HR, and senior executives has revealed that many businesses struggle or show little interest in identifying skill gaps, particularly for senior leaders and midlevel managers.

"The most successful businesses approach capacity evaluation with intention and method."

A thorough competence or capacity model built on the organisation's strategic direction is at the core of this procedure. For instance, "strong knowledge of big data and predictive analytics" may be a crucial asset for a certain group of employees in an e-commerce firm.

The responsibility of leaders, the clarity with which they convey organisational standards, and the zeal with which workers uphold those objectives are all signs of a healthy corporate learning culture. Positive learning cultures may be found in cooperative and courteous organisations.

Whether or not current workers would refer their employer to friends who are seeking a job is a major sign of cultural health. Unhealthy learning culture is also rather obvious. There is constant mental conflict, and employees have little faith in any level of learning outcomes or initiatives.

At work, bullying and harassment are frequent, and the learning atmosphere may be poisonous. Worst of all, top leadership withholds knowledge of the company's business plan, leaving staff members baffled as to why they are acting the way they are. It may be a massive undertaking to change a dysfunctional learning or working culture, and many organisations are intimidated by the idea of taking it on.

A set L&D agenda consists of a number of strategic projects that promote capability growth and are in line with organisational objectives, such as assisting managers in creating high-performing teams or implementing safety training.

The timely and cost-effective execution of L&D projects is essential for gaining and maintaining the support of business executives. L&D departments frequently struggle with an excess of projects and a lack of funds.

To secure the necessary resources and support, L&D leadership must have a continuous conversation with business executives about projects and goals. A small audience is the initial focus of many new L&D projects.

When a tiny pilot project, like an online orientation programme for a particular population, is carried out well, it can have a larger impact when the programme is implemented throughout the entire organisation. As businesses experience economies of scale, the cost of the programme per participant decreases.

Employee engagement and adaptability to corporate changes are enhanced by the learning culture. Teams or organisations become less dynamic under a hierarchical-centralistic culture. Because subordinates who deal with actual operational problems on the ground lack the flexibility to contemplate and choose the optimal course of action. In the meantime, supervisors lack the knowledge necessary to act quickly and wisely. As a result, businesses struggle with rigidity and delays in the face of a continuously changing environment.

Even though individuals tend to forget what they have learned without frequent reinforcement, traditional L&D programmes are comprised of several days of classroom instruction with no follow-up sessions. As a result, many L&D departments are building learning journeys instead of stand-alone programmes. These continuous learning opportunities involve interventions like fieldwork, pre-and post-classroom digital learning, social learning, on-the-job coaching and mentoring, and brief seminars. The major goals of a learning journey are to enable learning to transfer to the workplace and to assist individuals in acquiring the necessary new abilities in the most effective and efficient manner possible.

Additionally, any issues that develop naturally acquire the authority to think and make judgments in a hierarchical-centralistic society. Employees merely comply with task directions and accept judgments. As a result, the corporate culture has to change from one that is hierarchical and centralistic to one that is learning-based. It is crucial that we clarify the key distinctions between hierarchical-centralistic and learning cultures.

The psychological or power difference between superiors and deputies is present in hierarchical-centralistic cultures. Because leaders consider subordinates as inferiors, subordinates are unable to freely communicate their opinions with them. Then leaders have a propensity to shut down subordinates' ideas.

In hierarchical, centralistic cultures, there is frequently a reluctance to provide the team at work, especially supervisors, with critical criticism for fear of upsetting them. Communication in hierarchical, centralistic cultures truly cares more about the proper means to express thoughts than the underlying intentions and aims.

People are more likely to trust you if you have established ties with them. Trusting someone you recently met or with whom you had a bad connection in the past is difficult. To attain objective and factual thinking in a hierarchical-centralistic culture, individuals constantly avoid conflict.

Could you identify apparent signs of organisational learning?

Four signs may be seen in the company's learning activities, which show that learning has become a culture. The width indication comes first. The majority of employees in the organisation participate in learning activities, not just one or two. They are drawn from various organisational levels and roles. The depth indication comes in a second. Learning activities are not spontaneous or transient behaviours; rather, they have developed into habits or even taken on a permanent identity. The integration indicator comes in third. The company's key systems have been connected with learning activities. The structural stability indicator comes in fourth. There will be constant learning going on. No matter who the company's chief executive officer is or who joins or leaves the organisation, learning activities are regularly carried out across the board. The notion of learning culture, which is derived from the sociology of culture, is used to describe corporate culture in management.

How to build a sustainable learning system?

According to me, for a learning system to be sustainable, four key functions must be taken into account: adaptation, which addresses how the learning system's resource needs can be met; goal attainment, which addresses how the learning system as a whole sets a common goal and makes it happen; integration, which addresses how the learning system maintains solidity and coordinates to achieve common goals; and latency, which addresses how the learning system creates, maintains, and transmits relevant information. The latency function, which is how businesses develop, preserve, and transmit important value systems to all current and prospective workers, is a component of organisational learning culture.

The learning performance of the employees is impacted by organisational learning resources, which is significantly influenced by transformational leadership. Individual talents, particularly those related to exploration, exploitation, and individual innovation, are positively and significantly impacted by organisational learning cultures.

Numerous studies have demonstrated the value of learning culture as a corporate culture, showing that it affects employees' learning agility as well as work engagement. Employees will benefit from learning cultures not just by being more involved with the business over time, but also by being more adaptable to disruptive changes and continual change.

What incredible learning is taking place right now in your organisation?

You could have a staff member in one area who is having trouble and discover an excellent internet resource that can help them. In another, a manager helps his or her team members develop their skills by giving them some very excellent coaching. And in another, two coworkers collaborate to develop a novel response to a challenge. They high-five each other and continue moving forward. Make those teaching moments more apparent and communicable to others. By encouraging information sharing, you can make the most of those unique insights, advancements, and innovations and make them accessible to everyone. Additionally, you show that your company appreciates and supports learning of all kinds.

According to research, knowledge sharing is a key differentiator between high-performing firms and the rest, with their employees exchanging information at a rate that is four times higher than that of employees in lower-performing organisations. There are several strategies to facilitate information exchange. Three specific aspects of the learning process subsystem require special attention: the level of learning, which includes individuals, teams, and organisations; the type of learning, which includes anticipatory, adaptive, and/or action learning; and the learning skills, which include systemic thinking, mental models, personal mastery, independent learning, and dialogic processes. The earlier scholars each had their own interpretations of learning culture.

A report from Deloitte identifies a number of significant trends in workplace learning environments that are sustainable, including integrating workers' physical, mental, financial, and social health into the design of work itself, creating teams and superteams that use technology to enhance natural human working styles, and developing and acting on forward-looking insights using real-time data to harness workforce potential.

Perhaps most significantly, they point out that a crucial component of sustainable learning cultures is capitalising on worker autonomy and choice as the tools to foster learning, flexibility, and impact. Unsurprisingly, long-term outcomes are more likely when learners have control over their professional growth.

The key components of an environmentally friendly workplace are outlined in Deloitte's Human Capital Trends study. According to their research, 39% of respondents think that "introducing collaboration platforms" is essential to creating a sustainable workplace, while 36% think that "allowing for personal freedom in selecting how work is done" is essential.

Learning new skills is only one part of creating a pipeline of fully qualified leaders. In order to achieve tangible business outcomes like more sales, lower turnover, and increased market share, you must promote your company's learning strategy. Although learning is crucial for business success and employee satisfaction, knowledge workers barely devote five minutes each day to it on average.

Can an employee incorporate learning into each day of work?

When finishing things, be conscious and in the moment. While you pause in your job, ask your supervisor or coworkers about their current projects. Because of all of these inquiries, you now have new opportunities to learn and try new things. Make a list of things you need to learn. A to-learn list allows you the opportunity to list all of the subjects you are interested in learning more about, just like a to-do list does. You may then cross items off your list one at a time while taking concrete measures along the way.

Limit the number of extremely valuable, industry-or topic-related newsletter subscriptions you have. Make it a habit to read the articles that interest you every day and to research any subject or piece that needs further information. Learning in the workplace ultimately benefits both individuals and businesses. View the complete article here.

"Learning is the gateway to optimal life experiences. Learning transforms people's lives, and teaching, in any forum, is the art and science of bringing out the brilliance that drives those transformations."

Ideally, the organisation where you work is an exception. If you do, that may be extraordinary! But despite the fact that many people's demands for learning and growth may be obvious, addressing them may not be a top priority. Any executive will almost definitely respond with an affirmative "Of course" when asked if they believe in learning and growth. It is quite significant. The identical question posed to stakeholders will get a similar reaction. The top financial managers will be far more careful in their replies if you ask them the same question. Although we now understand that spending money on employee engagement through learning may result in measurable financial benefits, the same is not yet accepted for spending money on more extensive learning and development.

Even though it may seem obvious, doing basic things like prioritising learning, encouraging learner cooperation, and developing individualised learner development plans may significantly contribute to the formation of a lasting learning culture. These results present a future-looking view of sustainable learning cultures. In order to decrease burnout and improve sustainability, it appears that organisations must address employee health holistically. At the same time, obstacles to open communication and information sharing must be taken down. This is how you create a culture of learning. Which is why successful learning cultures matter.

"I talked about the effects learning cultures can have on luring and keeping top people, as well as the repercussions businesses suffer when they don't prioritise learning. I used examples of businesses that saw rapid development to demonstrate the link between these businesses' ultimate collapse and their choice to abandon "new thinking" in favour of a rigid commitment to the status quo." - Dr. Amit Das

The Implementation and Embedding Of Digital Andragogy In Organisational Culture- Hope Or Reality

"There is mounting evidence that most LMSs are grossly underutilised and that people often only use these learning tools when they are especially motivated to do so, when a crisis arises that may be resolved in that way, or when they are already passionate about a certain subject."

Success is about keeping talented people who are eager to learn with a setup that makes that possible.

Leaders have informed me that they are extremely busy "from eight to late hours in the evening," which does not provide them much time to sit in a classroom, despite the fact that our research shows that immersive L&D experiences in the classroom still have enormous value. Many people also stated that they like to learn and practise new habits in a "safe atmosphere," where they are not concerned about their career trajectories being negatively impacted by their mistakes in front of others.

The L&D department aids in the execution of the business plan for many organisations. For instance, if a digital transformation is one of the company's initiatives, L&D will concentrate on developing the human capital required to make that happen.

"In today's increasingly virtual workplace, it is more crucial than ever to establish a virtual learning environment within your organisation."

Leaders at Tata Communications, a telecom network operator, sought to provide an employee training experience that was as simple and user-friendly as what customers get when using Amazon or Netflix.

How can you create a top-notch employee experience?

With that in mind, the business created its own digital learning platform and allowed workers the freedom to choose the timing and mode of their training. The endeavour was successful. For instance, just 10% of Tata's training was available online at the beginning of 2017, but by March 2020, even before the pandemic hit, 90% of its L&D programmes were provided online, who also noted that many employees even choose to complete their training on the weekends.

During the pandemic, mental health conditions substantially deteriorated for people all across the world. While long hours and remote work locations had an influence on people's personal lives, other factors, including the financial crisis, mass layoffs, and dramatic rise in unemployment—all driven by the weak economy and lingering uncertainty—exacerbated worry and anxiety.

Building a culture of care may at first appear more difficult, but an empathic company will be able to increase employee loyalty, keep top talent, and avoid wasting time, money, and resources on recruiting new employees. According to the Annual Employability Survey 2019 by Aspiring Minds, the majority of Indian engineering graduates lacked soft skills, which need "human" interaction and cannot be substituted by computers, rendering them unfit for employment to the tune of 80%.

"Soft skills are becoming the new power skills due to their rising importance."

The COVID-19 pandemic has forced Indian businesses to change the way they handle many elements of the workplace. This is known as the "Changing face of learning and development in India." Training new hires is not an exception. That procedure is still developing. The current learning and development approach revisits the issues of learning what, how, when, and how much. These inquiries are necessary not just to help companies adapt to the changes that are occurring right now but also to get ready for changes that will soon be upon us in the shape of new laws and technological advancements. While some major corporations have created their own learning platforms, many businesses now offer tailored training for employees through online learning courses provided by suppliers.

Businesses are crumbling as a result of what is being referred to as the "Great Resignation" because they are unable to attract the talent they need. Employees desire greater compensation, perks, flexibility (see hybrid work), and career investment. Never before have so many individuals realised how valuable they are as professionals in the workforce. It's motivating, but it also increases the difficulties facing learning and development teams. It won't be simple, but it is possible to deal with high worker turnover, a fast increasing skills gap, and productivity concerns. The company can usually provide employees with what they desire, especially flexibility. Since many senior professionals place a great value on employees who can adapt, reskill, and fill new jobs from within, flexibility and adaptability really go both ways. The pandemic has demonstrated that workers will take chances when provided, so all they need to do is present the opportunity.

"The goal of reskilling, upskilling, and cross-skilling is to maximise the potential of current employees."

With the use of digital technology, businesses may work together with other partners whenever and wherever they are on the globe to achieve sustainable corporate success. Digital technology not only facilitates collaboration and innovation but also enters businesses into the "VUCCAD" World, which is characterised by increased business volatility, uncertainty, complexity, conflict, ambiguity and dynamism. The merging of several established sectors is a result of the "VUCCAD" world. The lower life expectancy of businesses is one effect of the "VUCCAD" environment.

The technical talents that are currently in demand and will continue to be so until 2022 are mentioned on Naukri.com. The need for these IT skills is growing, as can be shown by looking at the employment market. These technologies have the promise of effectively advancing operations, introducing novel solutions, and facilitating wise and informed decision-making. In order to accelerate corporate growth, organisations must adopt these technologies and ensure that all of their personnel have the corresponding abilities.Soft skills are developing as power skills , which stayed at the forefront during the pandemic and are reportedly trending as organisations migrate farther away from in-person to remote working methods, are essential for individuals trying to launch, grow, or stay relevant in their professions. These abilities aim to make the working environment more productive, efficient, and collaborative and are essential for thriving in the "Modern Digital Age."

Success is about keeping talented people who are eager to learn with a setup that makes that possible. As remote work and virtual collaboration become the norm, collaborative, immersive learning is the key to success. Employees continue to seek online enriching, community-driven activities, such as online learning, which is another trend that is still going strong. Leaders need to be willing to use blended learning techniques to design relevant and interesting programmes. To accommodate different learning preferences and styles, these techniques combine instructor-led, self-paced, team-oriented training with live courses, hands-on laboratories, boot camps, and other elements. The success of the gaming culture is an inspiration for many organisations.

Globally, gamers have extensive social networks full of strangers who work together in-game without ever having met in person. As a result, executives are experimenting with cutting-edge and group-based learning techniques like live virtual strategy meetings and VR headsets for onboarding. Organisations should assess their learning and development goals for 2022 to make sure they are social and include a range of learning styles. Individualised instruction will assist the next leaders in avoiding turmoil.

Organisations have adapted to new workplace difficulties in a post-COVID environment, many of which revolve around how to manage a remote workforce. Corporate learning and development teams may have faced more difficult obstacles than any other department. In order to facilitate and support a high-performing, hybrid workplace, L&D teams were tasked with implementing new remote onboarding and training programmes; tracking team member productivity and performance for virtual teams; and identifying cutting-edge, unproven digital processes and software tools. More specifically, the C-suite leadership is interested in continuing this digital transformation in 2022, led by L&D executives, because they have observed the success of many of these novel, creative L&D methods that HR departments have undertaken.

According to the World Economic Forum's Future of Jobs Report 2020, the digital transition will require retraining for 50% of employed professionals by 2025. Additionally, it was noted that although technological advancement may increase the need for technical abilities, it will also increase the need for powerful skills.In fact, the research on the HR Jobs of the future revealed a number of new HR positions in this decade that include people collaborating with technology. Companies are reportedly prepared to recruit applicants without a degree as long as they have the technical abilities needed to flourish in the organisation, according to Glassdoor.

Your current employees will have to be retrained in order to use new digital tools and processes as a result of the digital transformation. Additionally, it implies that many conventional job types that may be mechanised will be automated, rendering certain employment obsolete. That also creates chances because new employment will appear as new needs become more apparent (i.e., think

AI professionals). A new emphasis on ongoing upskilling has been added to organisation-wide reskilling. Many businesses want to promote from within. Leadership training is one way to upskill. With the introduction of online eLearning courses from cutting-edge professional learning platforms like Udemy and LinkedIn Learning, upskilling has become simpler for the corporate sector.

"People get hired because of their hard skills but get fired because of their soft skills."

Technology's development and use have brought about profound and revolutionary changes in the globe. These adjustments have given businesses a better opportunity to generate and provide value for their clients. Industry has resulted from the development and use of mechanisation, electricity, and automation technologies. These technologies have made it possible for businesses to carry out mass manufacturing continuously, without pause, around-the-clock, seven days a week. The globe has also become industrialised as a result of recent Internet advances and the use of digital technology or cyber-physical systems in commerce.

The importance of lifelong learning in L&D to consistently bring their a game to work, employees must be able to grow their knowledge and enhance their abilities. As a result, businesses must offer them plenty of learning opportunities and, more significantly, promote a culture of continual learning. You are assisting them in realising their full potential on a personal level in addition to their professional development. For instance, determine, for instance, what presumptions or limiting ideas impede their overall development both within and outside of the workplace.

"The responsibility of learning has always been to help organisations navigate uncertainty and chaos in the world."
-Linda Cai Vice President,Talent Development, LinkedIn

People have prioritised flexibility and fulfilment as a result of living and working during the epidemic and the economic, social, and political turmoil. Organisations are reevaluating their business strategies, workforce models, values, and cultures, frequently in response to fresh demands from the workforce. They are looking for novel solutions to relate skill development to career trajectories, internal mobility, and retention. While simultaneously bringing a new sense of care and compassion to employee well-being, diversity, and inclusion, they are searching for novel ways that relate skill development to career paths, internal mobility, and retention. It is quite difficult to keep up with this rate of change. Success is created incrementally by utilising market research, soliciting the assistance and knowledge of colleagues, learning from leading thinkers, and, most importantly, advocating the idea that knowledge is the basis of all worthwhile endeavours.

"Our top opportunity is to quantify the impact and ensure it is enterprise-wide, so that learning can help lead the way forward."- Sean Hudson Vice President, Digital and Global Head of Learning and Development, Pfizer

LMS solutions combine the conventional methods of online learning into a single platform that system administrators can easily control. With an LMS, learning uses fewer resources, improves, and reaches a new standard of excellence. LMS is, therefore, a crucial component of an effective business that cares about the growth of its workers and, by extension, about the growth of the entire business. One of the essential components of HRIS/HRM systems, a standalone programme, or a database on a company's intranet is learning management systems.

However, it could take a lot of time for a learning Manager to cater to each employees's needs. However, because everyone has a different learning style and speed, the idea that "one size fits all" no longer applies. The AI keeps track of a person's past performance and analyses new data continually to customise the present learning material. The AI tracks each learner's progress, recognising their skill gaps and directing them toward the right resources. Examine Smart Hints and Automated Tasks. I have been able to enhance the LMS system with "smart suggestions" and automated task checking using artificial intelligence algorithms.

Learning management systems are a tool to coordinate information transfer procedures rather than a service for a select group of professionals. It is appropriate whenever someone needs to be instructed and gives its users fresh insights. With the right application, artificial intelligence can transform e-learning, although it can take some time.

In order to improve digital coaching, you may anticipate more investment in artificial intelligence (AI). Artificial intelligence (AI) is a developing technology that is being educated by utilising the vast amounts of data from every business to improve human intellect, identify patterns, and make predictions. If you apply it to learning, you can systematically share the institutional and practical knowledge that individuals already possess.

When predictive AI and blended learning are combined, the result resembles an ever-present digital coach. The need for digital transformation is essential, and all departments must develop their technological expertise.

Natural-language processing is one area where this interaction is noticeable. Machines will soon be able to comprehend and translate human language in both written and spoken form. eLearning was created to increase learning speed while preserving (or improving) quality. This might advance thanks to racial intelligence.

What an LMS powered by AI can achieve for you?

By enabling a futuristic approach to team member learning, artificial intelligence offers a plethora of advantages to the great majority of learning management systems. In order to promote individualised corporate learning in the most fluid manner possible, AI-powered LMSs seek to simplify the way information is provided to learners.

- Learning and development managers may pinpoint knowledge areas that require consolidation with the use of AI LMSs, emphasising and optimising key pieces of knowledge.
- Additionally, AI offers precise advice on how to select and present content in accordance with the requirements and interests of certain consumers.
- Any firm that offers educational services, whether they instruct employees or their own staff, must have a well-functioning learning management system.
- You may enhance your teaching services by developing a learning platform that uses artificial intelligence.
- When used properly, AI can automate and expedite content management, design individualised training programmes and curricula, increase learners engagement, and do a lot more.

- The challenge is figuring out which LMS activities may benefit from AI improvement.
- In this chapter, I cover how AI may enhance an LMS, a summary of the capabilities to improve, and my top recommendations for using AI.
- Teams planning to build an AI-based learning management system from the ground up or add AI features to an existing LMS may find this book helpful.
- Artificial intelligence is a helpful tool that improves and automates many corporate processes; it is no longer a flashy and excessively costly technology.
- You may employ AI modules that are capable of developing sophisticated, customised curricula and assisting users with everyday problems to accomplish these jobs.
- While creating customised reports and onboarding new learning curator and learners while marking and classifying educational information.
- A lot of information is gathered by an LMS on learners' development, performance, difficulties in the classroom, system bugs, etc.
- Although it might be challenging for a human to examine vast volumes of data, this information can offer useful insights to a company that employs an LMS.
- On the other hand, an AI system can digest massive amounts of data far more quickly than a person and find insights that are hidden from a typical employee. make the content more accessible.
- Additionally, it may evaluate employee replies, give individualised comments, and suggest training programs. And AI will complete it more swiftly and effectively than a trained algorithm or a person.

- By giving employees instantaneous answers to basic queries and assisting them in problem-solving, AI can close this communication gap.
- Additionally, AI may modify a given piece of information to produce unique learning sessions, such as those used for corporate training.
- Employees, unlike employees, don't have as much time to study, so they require brief yet effective leraning sessions.

Getting your learning programme properly is now more crucial than ever since best practises for providing effective learning to employees are always evolving. Employees now want learning and development to continue beyond onboarding and to be provided using cutting-edge, useful techniques and tools.

Because of this, it's important for you to keep your knowledge current, and tools like learning and development articles, ebooks, webinars, and podcasts may help you do this. Whether your goals are to launch your learning programme, boost learner engagement, or improve alignment between learning and business goals, I am committed to assisting you in achieving those objectives with the information, insights, and expertise I am constantly gaining. Some of the numerous pieces I posted have clearly emerged as readers' favourites among L&D specialists like you.

According to IBM's Global AI Adoption Index 2021, 43% of organisations were considering using AI in applications, while 31% had already used such technology. By automating repetitive operations and accelerating the processing of massive volumes of data, AI-enhanced software often helps organisations increase revenue or improve services.

When used in an LMS, AI capabilities may boost system performance and raise the level of competition for your product. For instance, an AI-based LMS can help you attain the following advantages: Automate clerical duties that are done often. Because of course planning, user monitoring, handling requests for technical help, and other tedious and repetitive tasks, managing an LMS takes time. The process of translating and culturally adapting material can be sped up with the help of an AI module.

Reading aloud, explaining, or recording employees replies during assessments can also improve the usability of educational products for people with impairments. This enables knowledge evaluation and real-time user help. With remote learning, employees sometimes feel cut off from their instructors in real time, especially during external lectures. They are unable to discuss the outcomes of the exam straight away if they have any questions or need to.

AI is capable of analysing a worker's skills, requirements, and objectives before converting current knowledge into a series of brief lectures. L&D Lead must work harder when an LMS fills up with information to keep it current, user-friendly, and compatible with a variety of operating systems and devices. AI may modify the material, identify which lectures would benefit from revisions, and notify instructors of this necessity.

Over the last two years, learning leaders have exceeded expectations by assisting others in making the transition to pandemic procedures, remote work, and hybrid operations. They may now influence how their firms respond to change and rethink the future because they have the ear of their top executives.

Leaders in L&D concur that L&D has increased its influence during the past year. According to a survey report 74% of respondents concur that L&D has grown increasingly cross-functional. 72% of respondents concur that L&D has evolved into a more strategic role at their company. 87% of respondents participated in some way in assisting their company's change-management efforts. 62% of respondents concur that Learning and Development will be concentrating on reforming or rebuilding their business in 2022. A turning point in culture is occurring. According to Glint statistics, individuals increasingly rank the possibility for learning and growth as the most important characteristic of an excellent work environment.

As they create the new standard, organisations that value continuous learning will take the lead across the globe. Additionally, workers who give their culture excellent marks are 25% more likely to be content at work and 31% more inclined to suggest joining their company. The message in the headline is very clear: learning fuels culture, and culture fuels motivated individuals who are inspired to innovate, please consumers, and outperform the competition. Fortunately, approximately two thirds of L&D professionals believe that their culture is improving. Learning and development professionals saw a strengthening of their organisation's learning culture during the previous year.

I've discovered that when employees feel empowered to see themselves as learners, they are more likely to address a challenge with creativity, optimism, and resilience. Although this method calls for a cultural change, it may be highly tailored to the person and the task at hand.

Since almost all training and work activities are now conducted digitally, L&D teams should start gathering data for the various components of their employee training and development plan. The many kinds of data that may be gathered enable L&D teams to:

- Track the development of L&D materials used in employee onboarding and training.
- Analyze the impact of various courses, teams, and employee training programmes on learning outcomes.
- Produce employee learning cohorts that divide various learner types into distinct learning groups to create tailored learning flows. This will enable team members to benefit from the employee training strategies that are most appropriate for their learning style or personality.

You constantly enhance the overall L&D tactics and content. To demonstrate the importance of employee learning, describe to the C-suite how their L&D methods have impacted the growth and overall success of a organisation. The improvement of the feedback loop between the L&D team and individual workers is another trend for L&D teams.

Employees that are actively engaged in learning have the most pertinent insight about how learning tracks at a business may be improved.

In 2022, expect L&D teams to keep closing the gap between their staff and themselves. L&D teams will be at the forefront of change adaptation throughout the remainder of 2022 and beyond. These teams will be responsible for reskilling, developing, and upskilling workers so they can adapt to the business world's shifting norms. Increasing diversity and skill sets in three major ways simply said, immersive learning is a way to transform everyone's mindsets and abilities, including middle managers, frontline supervisors, and all employees. Due to this, learning may be made more accessible to all employees within the .

While L&D is still tasked with creating high-impact, high-quality learning opportunities, it is also now given greater, more complex challenges to address, such as future-proofing whole businesses. L&D professionals must thus devise new methods of operation and practise ongoing prioritising. Given the growing worry over the skills gap (the difference between the abilities people have and the skills employers require), they also need to learn certain new skills on their own, such as stress management. Programs for diversity, equity, and inclusion are not universal across cultures. For instance, several businesses have begun using DE&I training in Asia and have discovered that the Western method is ineffective.

Opportunities to learn and grow; belonging organisational values; well-being assistance; collaboration In the last several years, a tonne of learning technology devices with AI capabilities have entered the market. There are some very creative solutions out there to enhance workplace learning, especially when combined with other developing technologies like virtual reality, augmented reality, cloud computing, and the Internet of Things (IoT). Personalized learning content via recommender systems, push content via chatbots, peer-based knowledge sharing on collaborative platforms, and the integration of curated external content (third-party content) with custom internal in-house content are all possible to test, while page-turner e-learning courses and the utilitarian LMS are here to stay.

Getting your learning programme properly is now more crucial than ever since best practises for providing effective learning to employees are always evolving. Employees now want learning and development to continue beyond onboarding and to be provided using cutting-edge, useful techniques and tools. Because of this, it's important for you to keep your knowledge current, and tools like learning and development articles, ebooks, webinars, and podcasts may help you do this. Whether your goals are to launch your learning programme, boost learner engagement, or improve alignment between training and business goals, I am committed to assisting you in achieving those objectives with the information, insights, and expertise I am constantly gaining.

A McKinsey poll revealed that 73% of participants agreed that reskilling initiatives increased overall employee happiness, in addition to a company's bottom line and staff retention. Increased IT training should thus be a top priority for firms in 2022 since it will benefit staff on both a professional and personal level.

Is immersive learning the best option for your organisation?

Immersive learning is a crucial part of DE&I and upskilling plans, though it's important to assess the business and learning objectives before choosing the right learning techniques for a company. When determining if immersive learning is appropriate for your organisation, take into account the following factors:

- Do you want employees to apply skills and behaviors, or do you want them to retain facts and knowledge?
- Is it about adhering to a set procedure, or are people being urged to make better decisions?
- Do you want to tailor the learning programme based on your prior knowledge and experience, or should it be

the same for every learner?

- Will you make use of the data, and in particular, do you require feedback on task completion and customer happiness, or are you attempting to gauge skill levels?
- Are you talking about essential human abilities or technological skills here? Examining the figures for job searchers also reveals some interesting trends.

Traditional team member input, meanwhile, has been challenging to get. L&D teams may use real-time employee feedback to ask participants in employee training courses for their opinions in short surveys or longer, more in-depth long-form response surveys after or during the session. Learning through in-app experiences, using knowledge bases, or learning on-the-fly all give special possibilities for L&D teams to incorporate quick, straightforward questions that gather crucial information on the effectiveness and value of their learning and support material. Every skill set is explored in-depth through immersive learning.

It guarantees their ongoing development, including soft skills like human-centered leadership, coaching, emotional intelligence, cultural sensitivity, collaborative mentality, and DE &I that contribute to an organisation's efficiency and equity. Simulations go much beyond conventional strategies like ticking the box to read the corporate DE&I policy or going to sensitivity training sessions. Through the use of actual events, immersive learning helps to inculcate new viewpoints and habits while quickly exposing weaknesses and flaws. As a result, there is inclusive, collaborative, and empathic leadership and employees. There is no requirement that employees take coursework depending on their roles. Instead, new hires and those just starting out in their careers can progress from beginner to mastery with the help of immersive learning and practice.

In essence, this equips the workforce with new abilities to "future proof" it. bringing about change immediately and worldwide. Even while role-playing workshops could be seen as immersive, they can be expensive given that they only include a small number of employees at a time. On the other hand, immersive simulations may be distributed widely and rapidly to tens of thousands of people throughout the whole organisation and worldwide.

How to close your organisation's skills gap?

Companies must deal with the skills gap today because in the next five years, more than half of the world's workforce will require new abilities. Focusing on employees training has a big influence on culture, development, and productivity. The skills gap is not a new occurrence, but it has become more obvious as hybrid work has grown in popularity and made cooperation increasingly harder. Damaging talent will only make the Great Resignation/Reshuffle problem worse, making it a danger to the economic recovery of your organisation while it is still in process. The most effective strategy to deal with and close the skills gap is to harness the strength of your L&D department. You'll be able to increase employee engagement, corporate reputation, and overall company growth as a result.

The 87 million millennials in the US are only 56% white, compared to 72% of the 76 million members of the baby boomer generation, making the millennial and Gen Z generations the most diverse in history, according to CNN Money. From information exchange and e-learning to seminars, companies have attempted a variety of techniques in the past to transform a culture and promote diversity and inclusion, each with varying degrees of success. A new strategy is now required to successfully achieve diversity, equity, and inclusion (DE&I) goals in the workplace of the future.

"Immersive learning has emerged as a potent driver for achieving these objectives as digitalization has accelerated."

There has never been a better moment for businesses to take a close, hard look at their present skills shortfall since, according to the World Economic Forum, over half of the world's workforce will require new skills over the next five years. Beginning now is planning for the future. Any healthy business has always prioritised employee development. However, for a very long time, employees training was mostly something that happened once or twice a year, either through guest lecturers or at workshops and seminars.

Naturally, some businesses have already shifted to online training, employing an LMS as a content hub. However, the usage of such online training technology has risen with the shift to remote and hybrid employment. Companies must enhance their L&D expenses in order to benefit both themselves and their employees as a result of the pandemic's effects on the modern workplace.

"The skills gap still exists despite the fact that moving to online training and raising the money for it have greatly improved accessibility, diversity of material delivery, and training participation."

A recent poll found that more than 50% of HR managers concur that their firm is experiencing a skills gap. 51% of HR managers asked said they would rather train current employees than hire new ones, compared to 32% who were using new hires and 17% who were using independent contractors or freelancers.

In addition to being more sustainable than continuously employing new employees or depending on freelancers, training your current workforce is also a wise investment in the long-term success of your business. You need employees who can develop together with you, who have a desire to go up the corporate ladder and support internal promotions.

In order to develop new competences among employees and address the skills gap, upskilling and reskilling are gradual processes. According to the same SHRM report, half of HR leaders will provide upskilling (59%) and reskilling (55%) training to their employees.

However, there is another connection to employee retention that merits attention in this situation: 86% of HR managers believe that training helps to keep workers. This information is especially eye-opening amid the Great Resignation era, when keeping staff seems tougher than ever. Employees (82%) believe that training is beneficial to their professional development and job satisfaction (75%).

More than 74% of respondents believe they are more inclined to remain with an organisation that provides ongoing training, and 66% think training increases their loyalty to the employer. Promoting from the inside seems to be a terrific strategy for HR managers to keep and nurture that employee's business loyalty after employing training to close the skills gap.

By concentrating on your L&D department, you can provide your staff with the skills they need to succeed at work. Investing twice as much in training boosts performance, loyalty, employee happiness, and business culture throughout your whole organisation. These elements of your company are what really count, after all.

Due to the growth of eLearning, corporate L&D teams now need to regularly generate, monitor, and update their learning content. With in-app experiences, the core theme of the L&D trends I've examined is still digital transformation. Thanks to in-app experiences, L&D teams can produce learning, onboarding, training, and general support content that is integrated right inside the digital products that their workforce uses. This kind of learning and development (L&D) and support information enables workers to learn while doing their task, at the precise time they need it, without abandoning their digital tools. This kind of training reduces total training and onboarding time, increases worker productivity by providing the appropriate support material at the appropriate moment, and is more participatory and engaging.

Continuous learning has advantages for both employees and employers. The way to close the skills gap appears to be via training, particularly retraining and upskilling. But employee training accomplishes more than that. Training significantly affects a variety of characteristics of a business, including productivity (90%), growth (85%), and corporate culture, according to the recent poll of HR managers (83%). You already know that a worker who is comfortable in their position is more likely to work more effectively, to believe more strongly in the company's objective, and to contribute significantly to its culture.

Making the online learning experience emotive and relevant allows the employee to see the possible effects of their words, deeds, and decisions on their clients or coworkers. For instance, if a learning role-play is relevant, the learner will be able to picture the disappointment on a colleague's or maybe their supervisor's face.

Additionally, it's probable that the learner may witness or hear words of support and encouragement; these cues have been shown to act as diverse emotional state triggers. It's possible that the virtual high-five won't actually look like a high-five.

However, using immersive simulation, it is feasible to utilise authoring tools to produce realistic films, such as those of an employee's coworkers at work, which gives the learner a highly lifelike impression of the virtual engagement. The information must be relatable in order to be about people and people skills.

According to my statistics, L&D professionals may feel unprepared and are actively pursuing leadership, business, and data abilities on par with or even exceeding conventional L&D talents. The successful L&D function of today must emerge and instead expanded itself horizontally, out of its vertical silo around the company. Working closely with them entails executives, departmental leadership, and HR counterparts creating a learning plan with all minds. There might be many miles between you and this goal.

Top L&D executives are thorough; they have already made the first step planners who advance their education budgets from a variety of sources. They keep abreast of current events. Taking place in many teams and the many areas where L&D are located, can aid larger regional and local projects. An important lesson from these changing times is that the best person to understand what workers need and want is the employees themselves. Employee engagement surveys have become more popular among L&D professionals as a way to measure the effectiveness of their initiatives.

Over the past year, more companies have used more regular surveys to actively monitor employee attitudes. Additionally, just 20% of learners concur that their "organisation's leadership appreciates learning more now than ever before," according to this year's Workplace Learning Report poll. Make sure learning is front and centre in office conversations right now. Avoid waiting for a company or client to specify their needs. Determine what is going on outside and how it may affect your company and its employees. Future-proofing skills, suggesting learning technologies, and communicating the benefits of learning to leaders should be the main priorities of L&D.

People may feel uneasy, angry, and insecure when their weaknesses are exposed in public, politically correct language is stressed, or awkward conversations are poorly mediated. "Psychological safety is fundamentally built on diversity and inclusiveness." However, selling it as a means of improving performance is helpful. People are more interested in possibilities to improve and succeed than they are in corrective action that will make them seem bad. L&D is now experiencing a tough moment. L&D departments are expected to take the lead on some rather high-level projects, such as upskilling and mobility.

How would AI be embedded in LMS?

Management of learning A particular management system with a staff training component is called the Learning Management System (LMS). The LMS system includes simplified administration procedures, tracking of results, and sophisticated reporting in addition to improved documentation management. Training is conducted digitally, which is very helpful for individuals who work from home.

Training for new employees is crucial to the success of any business. Companies can handle instructional content much more easily and more efficiently using an LMS. There are two primary LMS types: Client LMS A system like this is put on the owner's server, and it provides users who are connected to this platform with access to training. This was the first sort of LMS to be created, and it is still used extensively for university students. Large businesses that require total control over the system and its procedures frequently choose it. Large and mid-sized businesses who seek to enhance corporate learning as well as private online schools use it due to its simplicity and usability.

In e-learning, AI is extremely important. Artificial intelligence is able to examine the kind of material consumers enjoy and consume since it is becoming more aware of what users believe and do. Additionally, it can now process data and deliver customised solutions. For instance, some LMS platforms powered by AI now provide customers advice on which courses to take to fill in knowledge gaps and deliver essential material on the specified topic. Artificial intelligence has a big impact on e-learning. We will discuss what a contemporary LMS is, how AI may enhance LMS, and the benefits for users in this post.

Cloud LMS Content is posted to the LMS platform server, where it is accessible to both the owner and users through the Internet. The most popular kind of platform for remote learning is this one.

How often did employees want to communicate with their leraning officer in their own language? Or to converse in their preferred language with an online learning platform? These wishes can be fulfilled by AI.

Furthermore, LMS training is accessible to both regular employees and newcomers throughout the onboarding process. Because of this, an LMS is a useful tool that improves training and onboarding effectiveness while using less time and money on learning programmes. The three words that make up the acronym are: learning, You may construct a single database of online training courses and resources using an LMS. This database is a veritable knowledge vault on your subject.

Your company's internal expertise grows thanks to LMS, enhancing its effectiveness. Management. The chosen admins are in charge of the training. They give out homework assignments, offer tests, and assign classes. system. The LMS audits the exams independently and keeps track of each user's study time. It is now simpler to evaluate the progress of an employee's training thanks to the system's analysis of all the data and the provision of a summary report. The LMS is widely used by both large corporations and mid-sized businesses because it allows for the training of not only a small number of individuals but also thousands of employees anywhere in the world.

How to maximise the outcome of an AI-based LMS?

AI offers workers immediate support. AI may operate as a virtual instructor by responding to questions, greatly simplifying the entire learning process. The inability to dismiss concerns as quickly as they enter our brains is one of the key issues with learning. Sometimes, "fear of seeming foolish" prevents employees from asking leraning manager for help because they are too insecure to do so. If employees ask questions that can be immediately addressed, the process of learning will be made more difficult. Every time there is a tiny bit of difficulty or uncertainty during the learning process, it is feasible to skip asking professors or searching online for the correct answer by incorporating AI into e-learning courses.

- Learners only need to ask AI a question to receive the required response. AI addresses issues with content and language.
- A branch of artificial intelligence called "natural language processing" aims to make it possible for computers to comprehend and process human languages.
- People frequently pick up new skills in a foreign language. It is impossible to develop a learning programme in every widely spoken language since the mother tongue relies on the country in which the person was raised. Too much time and effort is required.
- Once you have connected your e-learning courses with the AI assistant, people will be able to inquire about information and provide clarification in their chosen language.
- Learning will become a lot simpler and quicker as a result, increasing its allure and usefulness. Users may access material in their preferred language thanks to AI.
- AI improves the accessibility of content. AI also significantly helps those who are disabled. Take Microsoft Seeing AI, for instance. This open-source programme employs artificial intelligence to assist the blind. Texts can be read, signs can be recognised, scenes can be described, currencies can be defined, and individuals can be recognised in front of you, right down to the expressions on their faces.
- AI has a significant potential impact on how employees with impairments are trained.

- AI may be used to transform spoken words into transcription, making it easier for hearing-impaired people to comprehend a discussion's topic.
- AI aids in the creation of original material. In terms of creating fresh material, there are constantly new developments and successes in the field of AI. For instance, the title and the whole soundtrack of the short sci-fi movie Sunspring were entirely composed by AI.
- However, this is little in comparison to what could occur in the upcoming years. It's interesting to note that AI is already being used to query current online learning materials. In the near future, AI will be used to create all of the content for an online course, making the job of the professors easier.
- AI supports individualised instruction. Each student receiving the same material is a highly popular strategy in corporate learning.
- AI enables us to create adaptive tests that go beyond the conventional Q&A structure. AI can evaluate each learner's progress and level of ability, and it can then customise the course material for that student.

Making an organisation data-driven through the process of "datafication," which involves turning social action into quantitative data, It entails employing connected devices to gather (new) data from numerous sources and processes, or it involves building comprehensive consumer profiles. Making your environment, office, procedures, and goods smart is the first step in data-fying your business.

Previously "invisible" processes will become traceable as a result, allowing for better monitoring, analysis, and optimisation. The ability to make these processes smarter and assist you in capturing data consistently and universally across various processes, products, and workplaces has become easier and more affordable as a result of falling sensor costs, rising low-cost bandwidth, the affordable availability of cloud computing and processing capacity, as well as numerous connected devices.

"Digitalisation and datafication are the driving forces behind the future of employment."

If the learning process is not simple and engaging, learners won't pay attention in today's overly digitalised hybrid/remote workplace. Encourage ongoing learning and encourage others to frequently share what they are learning. Create "learning circles" where individuals may expand their horizons and inspire unforeseen creativity.

In order to lower barriers for employees, traditional L&D indicators like ease of access to learning content and course completions were created. These ought to be taken for granted. Businesses should relocate to the These ought to be taken for granted. Businesses should strive to foster the personal transformations that each employee defines for themselves. In other words, executives must declare that they "think that our business will grow as long as our employees are successful."

"Learning organisations where people continually expand their capacity to create the results they truly desire, where new and expansive patterns of thinking are nurtured, where collective aspiration is set free, and where people are continually learning how to learn together."

-Peter Senge

The key is to embrace the flow of work and life within the new normal in the end. Learning new abilities for the workplace will allow progress to become more organic, intuitive, and individual. Upskilling your employees, fostering a culture of highly accessible social learning, and coaching learners in leadership skills that they can use whenever and wherever they choose can help you reach the next level of productivity and efficiency.

Initiatives for corporate learning and development frequently rely on coursework and learning management systems, which are insufficient. Through mentoring programmes, it is possible to speed up employee growth and transfer important information across generations of employees. Employee retention in 2022 depends on learning and development (L&D). Over 90% of employees, according to LinkedIn, feel they would be more likely to stay with a firm that invests in fostering their abilities and skill sets. Since technology is advancing so quickly and there is a growing need for workers of all ages to have new skills, current knowledge, and constant innovation, learning is now a continuous process.

However, the duties they perform vary depending on the generation. For instance, Gen X and Baby Boomers play a crucial role in learning and development when it comes to mentoring the next generation. Some people even contend that receiving mentoring is a much more efficient method of learning than enrolling in classes or going to seminars.

How can you make sure that your organisation adapts to the changing times as e-learning approaches disappear more and more?

This chapter will explain how managers may encourage knowledge sharing among their teams. Knowledge exchange for development and learning numerous aspects of learning information and abilities may be picked up quickly. A new administrative assistant, for instance, may enrol in a quick two-hour training on team management software.

However, experience is something that can not be gained quickly. And this is what the previous generations could not provide. Experience is frequently cited as the finest trainer, and this is especially true when it comes to learning and growth (L&D). People in the industry who have more experience are in a great position to mentor others who are just starting out in their professions by sharing their knowledge and providing crucial assistance and advice. Because of this, information sharing, which comes in numerous forms, is essential to effective learning and development.

How does knowledge sharing appear in a company?

Brands that want to develop client experiences as their main objective must effectively train their employees. Increasing the effectiveness of the learning management system is one approach to empowering employees and providing them with extensive training. The eCommerce industry is always evolving and finding new methods to "wow" customers. Due to this development, marketers are now able to provide value through service methods to even the most straightforward purchases.

Using a learning management system (LMS) is the best approach to increase the effectiveness of these strategies and improve staff confidence, which will benefit customers.

Purchase and usage are the two main categories into which brands and businesses often fall. Where the efforts are concentrated makes the biggest distinction between the two. Usage, as opposed to purchase, places greater focus on the user experience. Many contemporary businesses have discovered more value when they focus on usage rather than products, particularly the ideas of increasing demand for use, promoting advocacy, being aware of reviews, and making sure a superior experience is provided at every touchpoint.

Creating demand for useer, make sure you meet users where they are in your business, if you don't do anything else. For many, this entails offering top-notch educational materials and community support. Several businesses have used their LMS to guide their staff through professional development and training so as to empower them. I've seen this applied, for example, when an internal sales competition is started. To be eligible for the contest, employees had to finish a module. Employees were given instructions that included a note outlining important details, including the kind of material (ebooks, films, etc.), an expected completion time, and regular reminders that they needed to mark tasks as finished. The crew was pleased with the outcomes once the interactions were simplified with the LMS.

Make advocacy your number one priority. Your staff members ought to feel invested in the business. You will not only retain employees if you treat them like customers and prioritise their experience, but you will also instil a sense of pride in the company in them. Scavenger hunts are among the easiest and most entertaining ways to accomplish this.

Give employees a mission to locate certain information in the LMS, and when they succeed, they receive a reward. This encouraging feedback will increase employee engagement and help them grow more accustomed to the system's layout. Give them the chance to offer input as well. The system will rarely be flawless on the first try.

Usage just soars through the roof when you build a platform that is intelligent, hyper-personalized, open, and uncontrolled. There will be a significant change in the way we talk, walk, and dance. Some businesses have created training programmes based on their analysis of the abilities their workers currently have compared to what may be required in the future as a result of pandemic-related disruptions.

Employees are divided in positions between those that are developing and those that are sunsetting as part of the workforce planning process, and as a consequence, role-specific training was developed. The main things I'd suggest we concentrate on are digital mentality and agility.

To identify areas for improvement, scatter survey questions throughout the scavenger hunt. Pay attention to user feedback. Although you have little control over what your employees say to one another, you may foster a feedback-friendly workplace.

There has been a significant rise in logins and social engagement when users have installed forums that display user contributions and acknowledgement messages. Positive reinforcement from coworkers fosters employee satisfaction and makes them feel valued in their position.

Encourage positive brand interactions. You can foster a sense of community even outside of special occasions by inviting folks to bring in mementos from their childhood. All things considered, your LMS ought to be a place where staff members are free to express themselves and ultimately come to feel more at home in the workplace.

Additionally, the organisation aims to teach problem-solving abilities, an innovative mentality, leadership skills, people-influencing abilities, and the capacity for all employees to be emotionally resilient. As more workers have been working from home (WFH) and are less engaged with business than in the past, these soft or behavioural skills have become more crucial throughout the pandemic.

People have been confined by the WFH situation. Companies are especially interested in developing these skills in their managers by teaching them how to create informal relationships and engage with their workforce. All of our managers at every level of the pyramid are being taught these new abilities. Employees must acknowledge that continuing education is a must for productivity.

Many businesses increasingly evaluate people based on their "learning quotient," or capacity to continue learning, in addition to their cognitive and emotional quotients. Range is crucial in the society we live in today since we're expecting workers to perform many different tasks. Businesses must also contribute to the development of a culture of lifelong learning. The culture of learning should be considered by organisations. It must be more than a simple function or procedure.

How would you maximise the outcome of learning analytics?

Data is the centre of the universe, and it will be the engine for business. Some of the key principles that will drive business are predictive analytics, business analytics, data analytics, business intelligence, etc. Predictive analytics is an essential component for businesses, with the worldwide market size estimated to grow from $7.32 billion in 2019 to $35.45 billion by 2027. Professionals will have an advantage in developing a variety of tactics to defeat competitors and maintain market dominance if they possess tactical abilities in finance, HR, sales, and strategic marketing. According to Gartner, demand creation should be included in marketing plans in order to increase brand recognition and generate high-quality leads.

Did you realise that LMS is a rapidly expanding field?

For reference, the market is now worth around $2.6 billion globally and is projected to increase to nearly $7.1 billion by 2023. And it's not that far away from here. Even though the discipline of learning analytics is constantly expanding, it is still relatively new. It is accurate to claim that we are utilising various strategies, resources, and procedures from different academic fields. This eclectic strategy has both benefits and drawbacks. The benefit is that we may expand on established procedures and alter them quickly to try a different tool or strategy if something doesn't work. The issue now is that we still don't have a clear-cut definition of learning analytics or a method for implementing it.

In light of the foregoing, I'm going to give you a few examples of how learning analytics are being employed. Usage tracking is one of the most commonly used strategies. The data was collected using a learning management system, or LMS, and other comparable online platforms. There are several methods for recording user activity on a computer or an LMS over time that can be used as a source of data. When employees use an LMS, they frequently engage in activities like clicking on videos, downloading files, and participating in discussion forums.

What will constitute success for your learning initiative?

How many individual employees passed the exams, or how much did it cost to build and deliver? The idea is that success may be defined in a variety of ways. I have to define it for each learning programme you wish to measure as a result. Learning programme measurement expands on learner and learning experience assessment to gather information about the overall effectiveness of a learning programme. It is almost difficult to determine whether data will be pertinent for collecting without defining success. It is beneficial to use a logical model when creating a chain of evidence connecting learning experiences and activities to anticipated results or consequences.

A logic model might be compared to a road map that links relevant occurrences with the desired outcomes. You must gather information about every item you list on the road map to make sure it is measured. Ideally, you are now prepared to begin organising the data you require and possess a thorough knowledge of the many techniques for measuring and evaluating learning via learning experiences, learners, and learning programmes. There are several options for you to keep on studying. The two most urgent next tasks are to gather information without hesitation. Having a shared dataset will make it much simpler to derive insights, even though it may take some cooperation, time, and effort. And reconsider what constitutes effective education.

A visual dashboard is a useful tool for quickly comparing different variables and identifying the most important learning indicators. Predictive modelling is another way that learning analytics is used. In essence, it's a mathematical model that calculates estimates of the events that are most probable. The information would subsequently be shown on a dashboard with pictures. Users may view information such as how long each individual spends watching movies, whether they open or skip through files, and how other users have responded to their discussion threads. The users may then use these forecasts to determine if they need to take action in response to them.

Consider it similar to a weather prediction. It informs us if it will rain tomorrow and whether we need to carry an umbrella outside. Predictive modelling may be used in education in a variety of contexts. The most common method is to predict a person's likelihood of completing a course, then use that prediction to direct assistance toward those individuals in order to increase completion rates. Some more sophisticated models may consider information about the employees, such as their previous knowledge levels and experiences, as well as how they interact with the learning platform and content. These forecasts are not flawless, much like the weather forecast.

I want to reassure you that we are in this together and that I will be here for you at every step since this is a difficult part with many difficult ideas. Make yourself comfy and spend as much time as you need reading this book. It's for you. With that said, let's begin establishing the framework for your primary themes and how you'll use them to identify what contributes to the success of learning for both individuals and organisations. Let's start by defining learning analytics. In order to comprehend and maximise learning and learning's influence on an organisation's performance, data on learning must be measured, collected, analysed, and reported.

Analytical measurement, the simplest type, is the act of monitoring activities and recording values. There are several ways to obtain this data, most frequently through passive or active data collection. The process of gathering data via the use of technology or a specific system is known as passive data collection. In other words, it is only assessing activity that is already taking place independently of your actions.

Active data collection simply means making measurements with the goal of gathering data. Evaluation, which is the process of extracting significance from the data you've measured, is a more sophisticated level of analysis.

Evaluation may be defined as the process of determining whether the data points to anything positive or negative. For instance, the definition of passing on two tests could be different.

There are many categories of learning analytics bring specific clarity to those what and why questions. Different degrees of learning analytics complexity aim to provide answers to queries like what and why things are happening.

To make better judgments, the categories might help you frame your inquiries. Learning experience analytics is the first of the three types of learning analytics. Gaining a deeper knowledge of a particular activity or experience is the main goal of learning experience analytics.

Answering inquiries regarding use trends for certain activities, such as mobile applications or e-learning courses, is frequently the aim. Excellent instances of learning experience analytics include the need to find wasted learning or comprehend how learners go through a certain experience. User experience analytics and content analytics are frequently used to help continually enhance learning offerings. Consider some of the initial questions our friend the instructional designer might want to pose to their data.

Is there any interaction with the produced experiences?

Learner analytics is the second subcategory of learning analytics. These analytics are centred on the learner as an individual or as a group, with learning serving as the outcome. Learner analytics also looks into the behaviour of cohorts within an organisation, such as a certain department or a group of employees who are finishing the same programme.

When considering our new hire, it is likely that they are most worried about whether they have finished the necessary onboarding to start their new job. Learning programme analytics is the third and last subcategory of learning analytics. This combines learner analytics with learning experience to assess how well a learning programme as a whole is working.

Give team leaders and HR a live view of learning retention. Based on how employees respond to scenario-based test questions, proficiency metrics should be collected and shown by microlearning systems. This priceless data and analytics give HR, learning specialists, and team managers a real-time insight into how effectively or poorly their employees are acquiring important ideas. Proficiency analytics may highlight knowledge gaps throughout the whole business or point out particular areas where certain learners are struggling to understand ideas.

Keep in mind that learning isn't always the final goal. What happens next is the subject. Applying the foundations of analytics is critical, but how you utilise your new knowledge to persuade others may be even more crucial. Sharing numbers and data is insufficient.

You must employ them in order to tell an engaging tale. You should keep looking for the most effective ways to convey new information through speeches, presentations, and stories. Additionally, please don't hesitate to email me. I'm willing to discuss analytics or your efforts to better yourself and others around you at any time.

Do you see any challenges to a digitised and data-driven LMS?

Technical processes and procedures are obviously vital, but managing conflict, communicating effectively, and exercising leadership are the things that elicit the most emotional responses. The learning experience will be more emotionally engaging if the learning objectives are concentrated on those that entail the development and use of "soft" or human skills. Include an unusual aspect in psychology and neuroscience, one of the most researched cognitive processes is learning. Surprise is one of the elements that scientists have discovered over the past 50 years that affect or cause learning that individuals don't forget. Online education is not created equal.

When a situation or action at work positively affects employees' emotions, they also get enthused and involved. Traditional e-learning frequently fails to engage learners emotionally. Immersive simulations do, and a little introduction to science will explain why. Recently, this idea was developed to incorporate more components by researchers that are trying to understand the relationship between human emotions and behaviour.

Recent academic studies demonstrate that emotion can be crucial to teaching. All aspects of learning, memory, attention, cognition, and motivation may be affected. For instance, memories created during emotionally charged experiences are more likely to be retained by a learner than memories created during neutral or uncharged events.

A learner's cognitive flexibility, or how effectively they can adjust to novel or unexpected circumstances, may also be greatly influenced by their emotions. This may lead to the possibility that a learner's emotional state may affect how they interpret particulars or see the big picture of a situation.

Emotions can also have an influence on motivation, another facet of learning. A topic or situation may pique your attention more if you experience pleasant feelings, like engaging with a real person or a virtual character.

These kinds of intrinsic motivators have long been linked to social learning, games, and simulations. Negative feelings, on the other hand, may be a powerful extrinsic drive.

For instance, the fear of receiving a poor outcome or offending someone with whom one is interacting might motivate a learner to accomplish their objectives. The ability to learn can be impacted by a person's emotional condition. The implication is that an emotional reaction may be used to modify a digital learning experience, engage the user, and enhance skill retention and behavioural change.

The research has clear implications for digital learning: for learners to have a better chance of succeeding within an L&D platform, the experience should cause the release of emotions so they are motivated to begin, finish, and synthesise the content, as well as remember and apply the learning to their job. Because they elicit an emotional reaction that results in employee buy-in, skill retention, and behavioural change, immersive simulations are an excellent digital learning approach. By taking into account the science underpinning immersive learning's success, you can make sure that your team's subsequent learning experience is adjusted to promote improved performance.

Use these three tested triggers to purposefully heighten learners' emotions in your design. The only interaction in many digital learning alternatives is seeing a lecturer give a presentation and multiple-choice responses, which causes learner weariness.

Although the actual answers may change, the experience of choosing a multiple-choice response without then understanding why it was the right or wrong choice is always the same: there is no way for them to experience the consequences of their choice, so there is no way for them to practise their skills.

An element of surprise that will elicit an emotional reaction is created throughout the design phase of branching into a first-person learning experience. A situation-based immersive simulation makes this feasible. Designing many paths through the information based on user input is known as branching.

This may result in a number of unique, applicable role-playing scenarios. As participants grow used to a prepared presentation that forbids direct engagement, some brain regions become less active. However, when employees encounter a surprise, these brain regions reawaken, causing the release of dopamine, which transforms the learning process into an enjoyable emotional experience.

According to Gartner, 70% of employees say they don't have the abilities necessary to accomplish their jobs, proving that traditional learning approaches aren't yielding demonstrable results in either individual or corporate performance. Utilising scenario-based immersive learning, businesses may maximise behaviour change.

By allowing the subject to experience first-person, realistic workplace scenarios where their actions may cause either good or negative emotional responses from their virtual colleagues, a learning simulation platform offers a simplified way of promoting and developing emotional states in learners. Instead of using standard e-learning experiences, immersive simulations provide learners with a greater emotional experience that ultimately benefits the company.

How promising does it look for the future of digital learning?

The workplace of the future has arrived. Therefore, how can you equip employees to deal with the quick changes occurring in the workplace? The future of work has finally arrived as you negotiate the changes brought on over the last two years. Organisations are beginning to emerge from crisis mode and are beginning to think about long-term planning for the "new normal."

Many people want to continue using a partially, if not entirely, remote workforce. However, one of the most urgent issues for the coming year is how to retain the best employees now while developing a workforce with capabilities for the future. Organisations will continue to encounter many of the same difficulties as in 2021. The pandemic and the Great Resignation are still having an influence on the nation.

Therefore, good leadership and skill development are more important than ever. Here are my predictions for the learning and development (L&D) trends that will influence the next year and what will be required to equip today's workforce with the skills it will need in the future.

- If you don't invest in their talents, your top talent will depart.
- Keeping your workers alive is insufficient.
- Employers may keep top talent by retraining and upgrading workers to fill in any gaps in their skill sets.
- Employers are noticing that learners are speaking out more than ever about their need for professional development within their organisation.

Building skills and competencies was ranked as the top priority by 88% of organisations in the year 2021 for skilling according to Pulse Survey. The most successful organisations in terms of learning and development goals are those that provide employees with a way to meaningfully change their abilities along a clear career path. Here are upcoming learning and development trends to watch for in 2022 as more businesses invest in their L&D departments and initiatives:

1. The completion of these upskilling and reskilling courses might earn participants time off, cash rewards, or other rewards, which L&D teams can use to encourage internal workforces to acquire new skills.
2. Contextual workflows are used to lead employees through complex or underused capabilities of business software, such as Salesforce, Microsoft Dynamics, or other programmes, in order to help them become more proficient users of the technologies.
3. New employees are led through the onboarding process through interactive tutorials. Teams may discover solutions to troubleshooting queries using knowledge bases with searchable FAQs. beacons and tooltips that draw attention to recent changes, critical alerts, or incorrect field inputs.
4. There are embedded anonymous feedback forms that let staff members comment on the current L&D and support material. Learning in the time of need is becoming more popular, much like in-app experiences.
5. Due to the fact that it gives workers access to support materials while they are working, this form of learning experience is far more successful than traditional training. Because they are learning through practical experience while carrying out their everyday jobs, rather than spending specific time on "what-if" learning and development, workforces can become more

productive.

6. A Knowledge Management (KM) strategy is more necessary than ever with a scattered workforce. Many companies are bringing in dedicated knowledge managers from their L&D or HR teams to lead a KM program. The advantages include a more effective workforce; improved employee training and onboarding; and simpler knowledge transfer in the case of an individual leaving for another organisation or the retirement of senior leadership.

7. A company's process documentation, or comprehensive step-by-step instructions on how to carry out various internal processes, is the first stage in a successful knowledge management (KM) strategy. The next stage in this process is to arrange this information into an internal wiki or another searchable knowledge base. Without these systems for storing material, internal knowledge is dispersed over internal Google Drives, PPTs, or is passed among staff orally.

This sort of learning has been demonstrated to help learners retain more information than traditional methods of learning since it is more important, engaging, and enables employees to make the connection between the solution and the problem at hand since they have already encountered it.

The practise of cutting up L&D course material into little, digestible learning units—usually no longer than five minutes—is known as microlearning. According to research, microlearning may increase employee engagement by 50% while increasing information retention by as much as 80%.

Microlearning is a means for L&D teams to get creative with their learning materials. It can take the form of daily assignments, brief films, in-app tooltips or walkthroughs, and more. Additionally, L&D teams may encourage the completion of microlearning materials by gamifying employee education and training assignments. This form of content is also simpler to reuse and renew.

The idea of knowledge management is to create, curate, organise, and share crucial organisational knowledge so that employees can access and locate crucial information. In other words, it directs staff members to the appropriate sources for any internal inquiries they might have.

Microlearning places a stronger emphasis on timeliness and application than forcing people to absorb massive amounts of new material all at once. The spacing effect and the testing effect are two scientific theories that are based on an understanding of how the human brain learns and remembers information.

Over a longer period of time, knowledge is presented repeatedly through spaced repetition; the testing effect delivers scenarios-based questions to learners. Science has put spaced repetition and the testing effect to the test and found that they provide outcomes that are noticeably better than those of conventional learning techniques. Provide easy access to learning finding a solution that maximises learning experiences and effectively fits into current employee processes and technological ecosystems is another typical difficulty for L&D.

Today's HR directors should put in place learning programmes that can be provided inside workers' existing workflow and are customised to how the brain naturally remembers knowledge. Microlearning can improve current tools and methods and address numerous issues with traditional learning. In this manner, businesses may maintain employee engagement over the long term and actively combat "The Great Resignation".

Workplace learning initiatives should take into account how the human brain functions By delivering bite-sized knowledge that is meant to captivate, microlearning significantly enhances retention, competency, and engagement in comparison to standard L&D platforms.

In 2014, I started by asking CEOs about capability development. In order to learn more about the conventional training methods they use and their expectations for upcoming programmes, I added 90 L&D leaders from 36 organisation to my database in 2019. In the past, the L&D function has had some success in assisting workers in developing their talents and excelling in their current positions.

Upskilling has been L&D's key area of emphasis. Although change is happening faster than ever, a McKinsey study predicts that by 2030, automation might eliminate 800 million jobs worldwide. It's anticipated that employee positions will keep changing, and a lot of individuals will need to pick up new skills in order to stay employed.

My data, unsurprisingly, supported our initial assertion that corporate learning must undergo radical changes in the next few years to keep up with the rapid speed of technological advancement. Companies must put more emphasis on blended-learning solutions, which integrate digital learning, fieldwork, and intense classroom sessions, in addition to upgrading their training materials. Employees will take greater responsibility for their professional development as a result of the expansion of user-friendly digital learning platforms, signing in to take courses as needed rather than waiting for a planned classroom session.

My study reveals that many L&D activities, at best, have only hazy ties to yearly performance assessments and lack a defined strategy and follow-up to performance management procedures. Annual performance reviews are increasingly being replaced by regular, real-time feedback in businesses. The L&D role can aid managers in developing the abilities necessary to give development feedback in this regard. High-impact onboarding procedures help businesses retain more new workers and achieve higher levels of employee engagement and satisfaction. By assisting individuals in developing the skills necessary for job success, giving new employees access to digital learning tools, and connecting them with other new hires and mentors, the L&D department may play a crucial part in onboarding. Leadership in L&D must be familiar with key HR management procedures and work closely with HR executives. The most effective L&D departments use performance reviews' collected development feedback as a starting point for their capability-building agenda.

"Learning has always been limited to increasing production. Today, education also helps with employability. Over the past few decades, the nature of employment has changed from lifelong employment to one in which employees are maintained only as long as they can offer value to an organisation."
-Dr. Amit Das

Creating And Pivoting Your L & D Strategy In Response To The Situation- Hope Or Reality

"Whether it's giving a presentation, writing documentation, or creating a website or blog, we need and want to share our knowledge with other people. But if you've ever fallen asleep over a boring textbook, or fast-forwarded through a tedious e-learning exercise, you know that creating a great learning experience is harder than it seems."-Julie Dirksen

In today's rapidly changing business environment, an organisation and their employees must quickly adapt to new situations and never stop learning.

The world's workforce has been continuously changing over the last ten years for a variety of reasons. The mix of personnel is changing as a result of a more competitive corporate environment, growing complexity, and the digital revolution. Meanwhile, reskilling and upskilling are valued highly due to ongoing unpredictability, a multigenerational workforce, and a shorter shelf life for information. The transition to a digital, information-based economy makes it more crucial than ever to have a strong workforce. According to studies, a sizeable portion of the market value of public firms is dependent on intangible assets, including talented workers, great leaders, and knowledge.

Organisations must place a high priority on allowing employees' personal achievement via career growth in the context of the "Great Resignation", a time unlike anything in the history of work. By tying skill development to internal mobility, career paths, and retention, learning leaders can develop stronger, long-lasting programmes. Employees expect opportunities to learn and grow without limitations, managers who understand individual working styles and environments, and organisations that offer flexibility as a standard of employment.

I'll walk you through a multiple approaches for developing a strategic learning and development roadmap that will help your business realise its goals, carry out its plan, and uphold its core values. To begin, let me explain the importance of strategic growth.

I have discovered a number of perspectives for expressing and evaluating the effects of learning:

> ***How well does the learning strategy complement the organisation's priorities on a strategic level?***

- How will the learning strategy help the company achieve its objectives? For instance, how, for instance, will it shorten the time to market for a good or service or increase sales by 10% in a certain area?
- How much of the business is covered by the learning strategy? How will requests beyond the scope be handled?
- What method will be applied to establish priorities? For instance, a governance team with representation from key stakeholders will control the overall strategy, establish the criteria for making decisions, and have regular meetings to assess actions.
- How will outcomes be quantified, reported, and tracked? For instance, the number of managers who are "ready today" or the speed of competency. Ensure that the executive team supports your learning metrics!
- How will the expenses of creating and delivering the programme be covered? For instance, central funding is provided for programme management and development, while corporate funding is provided for programme implementation through an internal tuition scheme.
- What additional talent work streams exist or are being considered?For instance, how are onboarding, performance management, and succession planning related to learning?
- Which positions are necessary to support the learning strategy? For instance, if the present staff has substantial subject matter and teaching knowledge but has very little experience with instructional design, you might need to adjust the team's composition to implement the strategy.

- What capabilities of the learning system are required to support the learning strategy?
- How will employees access education, sign up for events, and monitor their development?
- Which reports will you require? Can the present system, for instance, deliver reports that support your KPIs? Its ability to give microlearning.
- Which cutting-edge techniques and tools will be employed to produce deliverables and manage processes? Choosing whether artificial intelligence is acceptable, adopting agile or design thinking as best practises, or simply choosing a standard development tool like Articulate are a few examples.
- How will the company find out about the programmes?
- Which branding guidelines will be followed? Will education, for instance, have a distinct brand that adheres to corporate standards?
- How successfully does the L & D department support colleagues in acquiring the mindsets, abilities, and knowledge they most urgently require? By evaluating people's competence gaps against a thorough competency framework, this impact may be quantified.
- To what degree does learning improve the organisation's general health and DNA? A starting point may be established using the McKinsey organisational Health Index variables.
- How well does the L & D department support colleagues in maximising their effectiveness in their roles while preserving a positive work-life balance? Big data access gives L & D units a greater opportunity to evaluate and forecast the effects of their actions on the company.
- What additional techniques may be utilised to "advertise" learning, such as department meetings and

town halls? And last, how will your plan be in line with business leadership? Early support is critical for the learning leader. Even better is to participate in the creation of the company plan so that your learning strategy is well-aligned from the beginning!

- How L & D teams can promote continuous learning and assist in creating a learning organisation?
- What techniques can L & D teams use to produce excellent learner and learning experiences?
- What strategies for immersive learning can L & D teams use to promote learner engagement?
- How can L & D teams foster a culture of lifelong learning and develop a growth mindset?
- How can L & D teams use informal learning to support formal training to create a connected learning solution?
- How can L & D teams transform event-based training into a continuous learning ecosystem?
- How can L & D teams promote constant learning and assist in the development of a learning organisation?
- What techniques can L & D teams use to produce excellent learning and learning experiences?
- What strategies for immersive learning can L & D teams use to promote learner engagement?
- What strategies for immersive learning can L & D teams use to promote learner engagement? How can L & D teams foster a culture of lifelong learning and build a growth mindset? Any organisation's success or failure is largely dependent on its attitude. A learning mentality is essential for the continuous learning mandate to be upheld and a learning culture to be established.
- How can L & D teams use informal learning to support formal training to create a connected learning solution?

- How can company executives restructure their whole organisation whenever necessary, quickly, and effectively?

In a similar vein, the Docebo report highlights collaboration and open knowledge sharing as essential components of sustainable learning cultures, noting that employees in top-performing organisations "share knowledge with their colleagues at a rate four times greater than that of employees in lower-performing firms." Similar to this, the Association of Talent Development considers that "providing time for learning," "personalised development plans," "establishing responsibility," and "using culture to attract new talent" are crucial elements of long-term workplace learning.

Although most L & D teams probably place high importance on developing a sustainable learning culture, success in this endeavour is difficult. Currently, just 31% of organisations consider their learning culture to be performing at a high or very high level; the remainder are in the growth stage. Here are some useful suggestions to assist you in taking the next step toward a sustainable learning culture.

With McKinsey finding that "excellent implementers were 1.4 times more likely than bad implementers to have change leaders who have personally led numerous change attempts," harnessing your leaders is wise advice for any type of organisational transformation. High-performing organisations are more likely to hold leaders responsible for highlighting the value of learning in the context of sustainable learning cultures.

As was already established, learners who have control over their education are more likely to succeed. Which would you rather have: someone telling you what you need to know, or someone listening to your needs and assisting you in developing a personalised learning plan? According to statistics, "allowing for personal freedom in selecting how work is accomplished" is the second-most crucial element in the design of a sustainable workplace.

Promote a culture of sharing by adopting a development mindset, by doing this, you'll break down barriers to communication and foster a culture of information sharing. This should be a top goal since, as was previously indicated, high-performing learning cultures exchange information four times more often than other organisations. Your learning culture will be more enduring. The more information is shared throughout teams, the more you will learn and develop.

While having a strong learning culture today is wonderful, creating one that will last in the long run requires careful preparation. Since the usefulness of skills is eroding, prompting a wave of reskilling and a move from hard skills to soft skills, having a future-ready learning culture has become more crucial for learning teams. Simply said, L&D teams must concentrate on future-focused abilities to guarantee the longevity of their learning culture.

What exactly are the stretegic advantages of organisational learning?

- Studies, for instance, have indicated that businesses may boost productivity by putting in place a social learning strategy that cuts down on learning time.
- Reduce churn while increasing employee satisfaction. A corporate learning culture reduces the likelihood of employees leaving, according to a report in Human Resource Development Quarterly. Additionally, they

were more content with their job and more motivated to use what they had learned.

- Employee engagement is influenced both directly and indirectly by the learning culture.
- By continuously learning and sharing information inside the organisation, it becomes simpler to respond to client demand, market conditions, and unanticipated external events.
- According to research published in the Australian Academy of Business and Economic Review, an organisation's learning culture contributes to contented workers who in turn delight consumers.
- You may anticipate that employees will learn and grow more than they ever have, developing their leadership abilities and elevating their sense of personal responsibility.
- According to studies, the results of corporate operations are directly impacted by an organisational learning culture.
- By reviewing the data, making corrections, and documenting new best practises, you may prevent making the same errors twice.

Unfortunately, the majority of L&D programmes ignore these basic facts and spend billions of dollars on what essentially amounts to knowledge exchanges that are rapidly forgotten. Carrying on the cycle Lean learning promotes the agility that offers businesses a competitive advantage in today's market, just like lean manufacturing and the lean startup did before it. It may be as easy as setting up an online marketplace or holding regular peer learning seminars to link employees who are prepared to teach certain skills with coworkers who want to learn them.

- Employees will be more likely to continue devoting time to the programme if peer learning is made more rewarding by being incorporated into performance appraisals. Give your employees brief, consumable learning opportunities, such as hour-long classes on subjects pertinent to their current issues or possibilities.

- *Do you have a growing employees but a tiny learning and development team at your organisation?*
- *Does your learning department have a restricted budget but want to retrain and upskill your employees?*

Your talent development strategy may include using a train the trainer programme. Initiatives to "train the trainer" might take the form of learning courses that provide seasoned instructors with the ability to present information like cutting-edge technology or novel sales strategies. Or, these learning sessions might be professional development opportunities that instruct people who are new to the learning industry or subject matter experts (SMEs) who have been charged with instructing others on material in their fields of expertise in training and facilitation techniques.

"It's unsurprising that we see more and more progressive organisations naming chief learning officers — as was the case with chief diversity officers when diversity was no longer an HR topic but a business advantage. Learning is not an HR topic; it's a business topic."

According to research, talent may only be useful for five years or fewer. The workforce is going through a cycle of almost continual upskilling and reskilling. Learning programmes for instructors and instructional designers provide them with the knowledge and abilities they need to give their learners the greatest possible learning opportunities. To remain relevant and guarantee that their work has the desired impact, Learning professionals must keep their knowledge and abilities up-to-date. It takes both art and science to deliver employees training that is successful and interesting. It involves more than just putting a instructor in front of a group of employees to assist or demonstrate a task.

"Learning is a process that starts well before the actual learning course and lasts after it is over. The facilitator for a train the trainer programme must be carefully chosen to ensure its success. This individual has to be knowledgeable about the subject matter and skilled in creating learning programmes, but they also need to be respected, experienced, patient, and enthusiastic."

According to the Talent Development Body of Knowledge, facilitators of learning programmes must also possess excellent leadership qualities, communication skills, exemplary listening skills, and emotional intelligence. Facilitators need to be aware of adult learning principles and have the ability to engage learners, in addition to these interpersonal abilities and their subject matter competence. In train the trainer sessions, participants pick up a variety of methods, best practises, and exercises from the certified trainer that they may use to make the knowledge more understandable and memorable for the people they will be instructing. Participants in a train the trainer course could also learn how to use technology, which is essential to how you work and learn today. However, behaviour change involves more than just the learner; it also depends on the environment in which they operate. Is the boss encouraging? Is there a chance to put what you've learnt into practise? The trainer also has to comprehend how and why training affects an organisation.

Participating in a train the trainer programme might also be a stretch objective for some employees, enabling them to spread knowledge on a subject they find interesting. They can function as a resource for the course participant or the participant's manager after the training by providing advice on how to put the knowledge gained into practise, such as through the creation of a learning plan.

Sustainable learning cultures tend to put people in charge of their own learning through programmes like personalised development plans, learning that happens naturally while doing work, and technology that enables learning at any time, anywhere. This has the potential to become a self-fulfilling prophecy over time, when learners actively seek out information and learning takes on a life of its own.

Getting your learning programme properly is now more crucial than ever since best practises for providing effective learning to employees are always evolving. Employees now want learning and development to continue beyond onboarding and to be provided using cutting-edge, useful techniques and tools. Because of this, it's important for you to keep your knowledge current, and tools like learning and development articles, ebooks, webinars, and podcasts may help you do this.

Whether your goals are to launch your learning programme, boost learner engagement, or improve alignment between learning and business goals, we're committed to assisting you in achieving those objectives with the information, insights, and expertise we're constantly gaining. Some of the numerous pieces we post each month have clearly emerged as readers' favourites among L&D specialists like you.

Long-term success adult learning theory and its importanceIt might be challenging to find the time and energy to continuously focus on your own personal development, knowledge, abilities, and experience, even if you presumably know it's necessary to do so.

In today's job market, the willingness and capacity to develop and adapt one's skill set are highly valued. You are frequently drawn to studying as kids by our own curiosity and desire to comprehend the universe. Proper business will surely benefit from tapping into this innocent attitude. Set aside a set period of time to learn. You won't be able to cite being too busy as an excuse if you arrange this time as you do for every other job activity. Pay attention to what you don't know.

Honestly assess your areas of weakness and come up with practical solutions to strengthen them. Attempt to help others. Your coworkers, managers, and mentors are all capable of imparting priceless information to you. Integrate learning into your daily tasks. According to the research, the second most significant element in job happiness is the availability of growth possibilities (just after the nature of the work itself).

Every business executive would concur that L&D has to be in line with the broader business goals. However, research has shown that this dimension is often lacking in L&D functions. Only 40% of businesses claim that their learning strategy is in line with their corporate objectives. Therefore, learning is not explicitly linked to the strategic goals of the organisation for 60% of the population. Due to antiquated methods or budgets that were created using criteria from years past rather than current imperatives like a digital transformation, they could not be in line with the organisation.

"Make sure your learning is aligned with business skills. Rather than looking at hours of learning and course-completion rates, instead focus on identifying what skills are lacking in your organisation. With that alignment and clarity, L&D can create a skill-building program that's in lockstep with your business strategy."

Organisations should evaluate how well individuals perform in each of these categories after selecting the most crucial competencies for particular activities or job descriptions. Interventions in L&D should work to fill these gaps in competence. The majority of corporate learning is done through a mix of in-person meetings and digital learning methods.

How would you benefit from your strategic mindset while driving the L&D function?

A mindset of learning while working is growing among corporate educators. The basic idea is to include learning opportunities into people's regular occupations. This learning takes place naturally in some cases. After all, employees could be required to master certain software in order to finish projects or duties. There can be opportunities to follow a mentor or a leader. In other situations, learning leaders would need to budget the time required to finish a class, for instance, and then immediately try to apply it on the job.

Changing an organisational culture to one that emphasises learning corporate culture may be divided into three categories based on how it affects employee engagement and learning agility: No Impact, Single Impact, and Double Impact. Four aspects of learning agility can be seen: mental agility, which is the readiness to use challenges, setbacks, and mistakes as a means of learning;

change agility, which is the eagerness to use changes as a means of learning; result agility, which is the capacity to maintain concentration while under pressure for an extended period of time; and people agility, which is the capacity to draw on the experiences of others and work with others. The effect of an organisation culture on learning has been objectively demonstrated in a number of studies.

A business culture that has little to no effect on employee motivation and learning agility falls into the "no impact" category. This corporate culture is what we refer to as hierarchical-centralistic. An organisational culture that simply affects learning agility or work engagement falls under the category of single effect. Employees in this group may be adaptable but not engaged or engaged but not adaptive. The two-fold impact of culture falls under the third type. That is a culture of learning. Corporate culture affects both learning agility and job engagement.

Additionally, a younger workforce is more demanding of its employers and expects professional growth and ongoing education to be standard. Therefore, learning culture also affects employee experience and engagement. It comes as no surprise that CHROs and their teams consider fostering a learning culture to be a key priority. Learning specialists recently gave HR exchange network their greatest tips for creating such a culture: A fantastic initial step is to educate the leadership on the advantages of education.

However, HR directors must also assist people in comprehending the value of offering learning opportunities. Education is successful whenever learning experts can show a connection between talent acquiring upskilling or reskilling and then going out and generating more money for the organisation. Educating leaders on the value of growth and learning is not sufficient. They must also be ready to devote resources to learning and development. According to me, leaders must "give an infrastructure and the ability to become a lifelong learner" in addition to demonstrating the growth mindset and behaviours associated with it.

An organisation must visibly and unambiguously comprehend, recognise, and promote the relevance of learning and innovation in reference to business performance and success if it is to foster a healthy, business-focused culture of lifelong learning, performance, and innovation. Employee interest in learning opportunities and professional development is undoubtedly higher than it has ever been. Some individuals, nevertheless, might not feel as inspired as others. Or they could feel stretched by trying to balance studies and work-related responsibilities. Personalised education is growing in acceptance as a result.

Job satisfaction and performance may both be enhanced by providing employees with the opportunity to develop in a way that promotes both their own personal objectives and those of the business. The keys to creating this learning culture are tailoring the learning path for each employee and tying the learning curve to the income curve.

Learning has always been limited to increasing production. Today, education also helps with employability. Encourage and involve workers. Giving employees the chance to grow and acquire new skills is the most crucial factor in employee engagement. Research reveals that happiness is influenced by lifetime learning. Highly engaged individuals are more likely to be inspired by new prospects at work and content with their existing organisation when they are given the ability to grow and develop within their chosen career path.

With the use of modern technology, you may customise learning such that it changes courses based on employee performance and adapts the content to each employee's requirements, learning preferences, and preferred methods of delivery. Assist continuously. After a learning session, giving employees further help via voice, text, and chatbots ensures that they can apply what they learned to particular problems. Engage in peer learning. When it comes to learning a new skill, 55% of your employees will seek advice from a coworker before turning to Google or your learning management system (LMS).This makes sense, given that people frequently learn as they teach. Learning by doing provides a technique to promote quick, just-in-time learning while enhancing the conceptual knowledge your employees already possess.

Organisations can open doors for unrestricted growth by matching employee skill sets with the an organisation's long-term goal. How learning road maps plays a part in organisations must set up an effective road map in order to foster a learning culture at work. For this, they need to be aware of the top abilities of their staff members and the significance of those skills to the business. After that, they should develop a strategy that includes tactics for developing these abilities using a variety of media, such as reading, viewing videos, listening to audio, etc. This will make it easier for workers with varying learning styles to understand all ideas in a consistent way.

The organisation may then begin to consider upgrading skills by comprehending neighbouring skill sets to the present roles and competencies and developing a learning strategy for each position and function. This has to be an active plan that is continually modified in response to market and technological developments. The appropriate partner may significantly improve the results and aid in identifying important market trends and a plan to become the best of the breed.

Traditional workplace cultures are no longer necessary since they cannot support the current pace of growth because they are too stagnant.They are constrained and prevent the cross-functional learning that the modern corporate environment requires. Therefore, a flat organisational structure that encourages learning is the only viable option. Over here, one may freely learn and improve in both quantity and quality over time.

In the end, businesses and the workforce will be divided into winners and losers based on their commitment to lifelong learning. The skills gap is catching up to everyone since the workplace of the future has already arrived in many ways. Therefore, fostering a learning culture goes beyond providing staff with a great perk. It's a must for business. Employees now, more than ever, need a sense of "meaning" and "worth" at work. Organisations may achieve twice as much customer satisfaction and innovation, as well as produce on average 25% more profits, when they prioritise the link between engagement and performance and focus on the employee experience. Given the talent crisis and the danger of automation, now is the time to take action.

How can L&D teams lead the transformation of the learning culture and assist in creating a learning organisation?

Learn about the crucial role that L&D teams play in cultural development and about tried-and-true methods for fostering an organisational culture of continuous learning. There are many more ways to learn than the ones I've just listed. A few of them are listed below. This list is by no means exhaustive, though.

- Workshops and lectures, frequently utilise a SME and employees in this more formal atmosphere.
- Groups for discussion are a very interactive environment designed to exchange ideas.
- Debate is a highly interactive environment designed to persuade others of one's opinions.
- Projects and case studies that involve the participants directly and encourage them to provide ideas for answers and solutions.
- Experience-based activities that promote participation and are frequently used in team-building exercises.
- Play a role in order to train customer contact. For instance, a role is acted out or performed.
- Simulations or games are a well-liked and participatory approach to experiential learning. This may be made to appear quite lifelike with the development of virtual and augmented reality.
- Shadowing a job where you may learn from collaborating with a coworker who has a different background may be a good idea. This is a beneficial approach to learning and interacting.
- The expansion of outdoor management (OMD), for instance, is an experienced activity. Hamilton & Cooper's study from 2001 indicated that this may be successful. 50% of the participants reported significant levels of stress and poor mental wellness before and following attendance. It was determined that if the participants weren't under excessive strain or didn't have low levels of mental energy, a stronger influence might be made.

- Coaching the development of practical skills is a key component of coaching. The coach is frequently designated and acts as the driver. The coach learns by doing as they do.
- Mentoring The strategic approach of mentoring The mentee selects the mentor, and the mentee also controls the process. Mentorship extends beyond teaching skills. But there is a lot more than that.

What will you choose: mentorship or online learning?

Mentorship is one method by which seasoned workers may pass on their skills. A more seasoned worker is paired with a less seasoned one in order to encourage and mentor the latter as they mature and develop. Additionally, knowledgeable staff members can impart their expertise through training, which entails giving instructions and direction on how to carry out certain tasks or activities. There are several ways to give training, including in-person seminars, online modules, and e-learning programmes.

Mentorship is unquestionably the most effective strategy of the two for transferring information among the experienced and novice members of your organisation. But why is that the case, and how can it help your organisation? Why knowledge sharing through mentoring should be adopted by your organisation above all things, mentoring encourages the sharing of knowledge and ideas; it permits the open interchange of ideas with quick opportunity for clarification, queries, and feedback. There are other additional advantages, including "Organic knowledge and experience transmission." When there is trust between mentor and mentee, the transmission of tacit knowledge is more likely to occur naturally. In other words, if knowledge is imparted in the context of a supportive relationship, it is more likely to be kept and used possibilities to fix errors frequently. A safe environment is provided via mentoring connections for experimentation and taking risks.

Mentoring connections provide workers the chance to exchange fresh perspectives, which boosts innovation and creativity inside an organisation. Your business should start a knowledge-sharing through mentoring programme if you want to enjoy these advantages. This entails developing a framework that promotes and fosters mentoring relationships between staff members from various departments and levels of expertise. E-learning for L&D E-learning is one of the most overused and ineffective techniques of knowledge acquisition in business. Despite our best efforts, genuine learning cannot occur by spending hours in front of a computer watching movies and selecting the correct answers to multiple-choice questions. Globally, $359 billion is spent on e-learning each year, but most of the time, the investment isn't worth it, according to Harvard Business Review.

To summarise, while e-learning can supplement more traditional forms of learning, such as mentorship, it cannot replace them. This is so because human beings are hardwired to engage and connect with one another. True learning occurs when we are able to apply what we have learned to a real-life scenario, which can only occur when we are being mentored by an experienced person who can assist us in doing so.

David A. Kolb first used the phrase "experiential learning" a long time ago, and it still holds true in the modern corporate world. Learning has to be experienced in order to be effective; it also requires peer contact, cooperation, and feedback, none of which can be accomplished through an out-of-date e-learning package.

On the other hand, mentoring offers a means for all of these things to happen.

How can a mentor programme be included in your present L&D procedures?

How to connect staff members with skilled mentors? It is obvious that mentorship has a lot to offer businesses and that it is superior to e-learning modules in terms of interpersonal interaction and hands-on learning. However, it's not always obvious how to match staff members with knowledgeable mentors. When matching a mentor and mentee, the following factors should be taken into account:

1. Combine inexperienced and experienced individuals.
2. Although this coupling is arguably the most obvious, it is nonetheless significant.
3. Employees with experience may help newcomers to the organisation learn and advance more quickly by imparting their knowledge and expertise.
4. Additionally, when the mentee advances, they can mentor additional new hires.
5. Examine the mentor's and mentee's skill sets. It's critical to confirm that the mentor and mentee are a good match.
6. The mentee should be open to learning from the mentor, and the mentor should have the skills and information the mentee wishes to acquire.
7. Take into account the personalities of the mentor and mentee. To get along, mentors and mentees should have comparable personalities. Conflict and tension may result from personality conflicts.
8. Align the objectives of the mentor and the mentee. The objectives of the mentor and mentee should align. If they don't, it could be challenging for the mentor to

offer the mentee helpful advice and assistance.

9. After taking these variables into consideration, your next step will be to develop a system that makes matching mentors and mentees simple and convenient.

10. Creating a database of mentors and mentees or using an online platform that enables staff members to look for mentors and mentees based on their skill sets and objectives might be two ways to go about this.

11. Using technology to match mentors making a mentoring program automated larger firms frequently embrace automated employee mentoring programme solutions. Pairing personnel manually becomes a burden on the administrative staff.

12. Finding a mentor who is appropriate for each employee's goals, personality, talents, and experience requires too much time from an HR expert. In order to ensure that every employee makes a meaningful connection at work, mentoring software uses an algorithm to remove the guesswork from pairing.

13. Monitoring mentoring relationships is another capability provided by mentoring software to HR departments. The platforms offer session agendas that help participants stay on topic by focusing their talks on issues like goal-setting and professional progression.

14. The mentors and mentees are asked to rate and provide comments after each session. Program managers now have the data they need to assess the effectiveness of their programmes. They may receive precise information on how often pairings meet, what they talk about, how much progress is made, and how they feel about their match rather than just anecdotal input.

15. By using mentoring platforms, managers may concentrate on creating deep connections among their

staff instead of using time-consuming spreadsheets. It might be argued that mentoring the next workforce is what will ultimately decide an organisation's success.

16. In GP Strategies research, 70% of executives cited mentoring as the most beneficial way to grow one's talents, with coaching coming in second place. I discovered that 80% of workers wanted a mentor who had followed a similar professional path to the one they desired. You need role models, so that makes sense.

Why are hybrid workplaces and virtual learning so popular?

Organisations have been compelled to rethink, reimagine, and reorganise their business processes as a result of the epidemic and the rapid increase of digitalisation. These dynamic times have accelerated the transition to remote or hybrid work arrangements, in addition to fostering the adoption of digital technology. All of this had an effect on the workforce and its potential for success. It also brought about corporate losses, the "Great Resignation", and the requirement for skill upgrades in order to remain relevant in the face of changing global conditions.

Utilising a variety of skill sets has therefore become essential for the existing and future workforce. To remain competitive in the changing business world, professionals must be knowledgeable of the latest abilities. As a result, in order to be ready for the job market of the future, one must be informed of the most recent trends that have survived in these unstable and difficult times. New technologies and concepts have emerged during the past several years, and this trend of innovation is anticipated to remain for much longer.

In a society that is quickly virtualising and largely dependent on paper work, effective leadership has never been more important. By offering a personal mentor who can deliberately analyse strengths and enable the learning of new abilities to promote progress, coaching speeds up the professional development of leaders. As a result of the shortage of qualified candidates, developing leadership abilities must be a crucial component of learning across the organisation.

According to a McKinsey Global Survey on the demands of the future workforce, nearly 90% of executives and managers believe their organisation already suffer from skill gaps or anticipate skill gaps in the upcoming five years. According to the same survey, data analytics (43%) and IT, mobile, and/or web design management are the top two organisation sectors with the highest need to address possible skill gaps, according to the same survey (26%). The IT skills gap must be acknowledged by organisations as being present and expanding. Employees must thus set aside time on their own to acquire new skills and keep up with the speed of their organisation. Wherever there is a need, it is incumbent on the organisation to provide and support opportunities that retain people and scale capabilities throughout the organisation.

The effectiveness and impact of a learning approach should be assessed using key performance indicators (KPIs). The first indication evaluates the degree to which all L&D investments and efforts are in line with business goals. The second KPI examines whether learning interventions alter people's performance and behaviour. The last KPI examines the efficiency with which resources and investments are put to use in the corporate academy. Since accurate assessment is rarely straightforward, many businesses continue to use outdated performance indicators like satisfaction and completion rates for learning programmes.

However, high-performing firms put more emphasis on outcomes-based indicators, including the influence on employee engagement, teamwork, and business process improvement. Four lenses have been established for articulating and assessing the effects of learning:

1. Strategic alignment: How well does the organisation's learning strategy complement its priorities?

2. Capabilities: How successfully does the L&D department support colleagues in acquiring the mindsets, talents, and knowledge they most urgently require? By evaluating people's competence gaps against a thorough competency framework, this impact may be quantified.

3. The general health and DNA of the organisation are strengthened by learning in what ways? A starting point may be established using the McKinsey organisational Health Index variables.

4. Individual peak performance: Aside from basic skills, how well does the L&D department support colleagues in making the most of their jobs while maintaining a positive work-life balance? Big data access gives L&D units a greater opportunity to evaluate and forecast the effects of their actions on the organisation. Corporate learning initiatives from L&D should be a priority on the HR agenda, just as they should be for the organisation. L&D is crucial to the workforce, succession planning, performance management, onboarding, and promotion processes.

The "70:20:10" paradigm, which many L&D departments use, states that 70% of learning occurs at work, 20% occurs via contact and cooperation, and 10% occurs as a result of formal learning interventions, including classroom instruction and online curriculum. These ratios are only averages; they change depending on the sector and the organisation. The formal learning component has typically been the emphasis of L&D operations. L&D leaders today must create and put into action interventions that promote informal learning, including coaching and mentoring, on-the-job training, apprenticeships, leadership shadowing, action-based learning, on-demand access to digital learning.

The most important technological platforms and applications are those that provide just-in-time learning. Virtual classrooms, mobile learning apps, embedded performance-support systems, polling software, learning-video platforms, learning-assessment and -measurement platforms, massive open online courses (MOOCs), and small private online courses (SPOCs) are a few examples of next-generation learning management systems. The learning technology market has completely shifted to cloud-based platforms, giving L&D departments infinite chances to plug and unplug systems and access the most recent features without having to go through time-consuming and expensive on-premises system instals. To support the complete talent cycle, including recruiting, onboarding, performance management, L&D, real-time feedback tools, career management, succession planning, and more, L&D executives must ensure that learning technologies fit into a larger system architecture.

Although fewer L&D executives have executed large-scale transformation initiatives, many are becoming aware of the difficulties brought on by the Fourth Industrial Revolution (technologies bridging the physical and digital worlds). Instead, most are gradually changing their approach and curriculum to suit the situation. L&D

executives must act now because human capital is more crucial than ever and will be the main determinant in maintaining competitive advantage over the next few years. This is because technology is developing at an ever-increasing rate. The leaders of L&D departments need to revolutionise their approach by developing a learning strategy that is in line with an organisational strategy and by identifying and supporting the competencies required for success. The outcome of this strategy will be comprehensive curricula that make use of all pertinent and available learning methods and technology.

"The most successful businesses will make investments in cutting-edge L&D initiatives, maintain flexibility and agility, and develop the human capital required to succeed in the digital era."

The majority of corporate learning is done through a mix of in-person meetings and digital learning methods. Leaders have informed us that they are extremely busy "from eight to late," which does not provide them much time to sit in a classroom, despite the fact that our research shows that immersive L&D experiences in the classroom still have enormous value. Many people also stated that they like to learn and practise new skills and behaviours in a "safe setting" where they are not concerned about making mistakes in front of others that may have an impact on their career pathways.

Even though individuals tend to forget what they have learned without frequent reinforcement, traditional L&D programmes are comprised of several days of classroom instruction with no follow-up sessions. As a result, many L&D departments are building learning journeys instead of stand-alone programmes. These continuous learning opportunities involve interventions like fieldwork, pre-and post-classroom digital learning, social learning, on-the-job coaching and mentoring, and brief seminars. The major goals of a learning journey are to enable learning to transfer to the workplace and to assist individuals in acquiring the necessary new abilities in the most effective and efficient manner possible.

Scalability and performance Several strategic initiatives that promote capability creation and are in line with business goals make up a defined L&D agenda, such as assisting leaders in creating high-performing teams or implementing safety training. The timely and cost-effective execution of L&D projects is essential for gaining and maintaining the support of business executives. L&D departments frequently struggle with an excess of projects and a lack of funds. To secure the necessary resources and support, L&D leadership must continuously discuss objectives and priorities with business executives. A small audience is the initial focus of many new L&D projects.When a tiny pilot project, like an online orientation programme for a particular population, is carried out well, it can have a larger impact when the programme is implemented throughout the entire organisation. As businesses experience economies of scale, the cost of the programme per participant decreases.

Almost 74% of businesses prefer to create their own individualised, learner-centric material through their L&D departments instead of purchasing it. Organisations are concentrating on building internal content curation skills and minimising reliance on outside providers. About 80% of businesses want to develop "content curation" as a crucial skill for their L&D teams in the future.

How does the AI-based platform recognise, evaluate, and adapt to the development of the learner?

Creating content in-house will help organisations optimise their learning expenditures, speed up turnaround, and deliver customised material for modern learners. Organisations are becoming more aware of "empathy" as a critical skill as they transition to human-centered learning methodologies. Acts of empathy, according to 86% of leaders, may give insights into the needs and feelings of others, resulting in the development and maintenance of strong working relationships, cooperation, and collaboration. Artificial intelligence (AI) has developed, shown up, and been incorporated into our daily lives.

By processing and analysing information or data to identify patterns, make decisions, increase productivity, and improve performance, AI technology is used to automate operations. In essence, artificial intelligence is a collection of algorithms that can produce outcomes even when they are not explicitly directed to do so. Some people think of artificial intelligence (AI) as a methodical process of replicating human qualities and skills in a computer while simultaneously using its processing power to outperform human capacity. It enables humans to make complex judgments with wide-ranging effects.

Artificial intelligence is defined by its capacity for logical thought and the adoption of strategies that are most effective in achieving predetermined objectives. Experts in learning and development work to research and apply AI to provide fresh approaches to training. AI may help planners create more efficient and effective training methods and approaches, which is the most significant way it can have an impact on the training, learning, and development industry.

Here are those practical ways AI can change how humans learn.

- While AI may be seen as just another aspect of learning technology, realising its full potential requires seeing customised learning from a whole different perspective. Without artificial intelligence, it would not be feasible to deliver individualised material in a way that accommodates each learner's unique tastes and learning preferences.
- In order to prepare AI to support individualised learning, it must be exposed to as many different variables and input data as is practical. Online tools that may close gaps and aid in learning objectives are necessary for learners.
- One approach to achieving this is to predict outcomes and to provide particular information depending on the learner's prior performance and personal objectives. Personalized recommendations that are specifically tailored to the learner's ability gap aid in knowledge development.

The following is a summary of some more advantages of using artificial intelligence in customised learning: Learning objectives may be attained significantly more quickly by presenting learners with tailored material. AI analyses each learner's goals and performance history before recommending a learning programme to them. The learning route becomes more immersive and interesting for the employee as a result.

AI may be used to create a learning programme where all information, timetables, programmes, and materials are based on the preferences and past experiences of the learner. The goals are kept track of and delivered. Programs that are more rapid, interactive, and immersive produce higher learning results, which have a beneficial effect on the organisations' learning investment. With the advent of artificial intelligence in the classroom, learning today is more sophisticated, efficient, online, and cross-cultural. The approach of material learning is reinterpreted with less reliance on location or practical learning.

"Artificial intelligence is used by adaptive learning systems to identify a learner's strengths, limitations, learning preferences, and level of competence before supplying them with the appropriate learning resources."

There are a few crucial ideas to bear in mind: the calibre of the teaching materials used. Tracking, evaluating, and levelling up performance depending on outcomes. Customised learning systems are replacing traditional techniques as human learning evolves. As more institutions adopt coordinated interactions, the value of AI in adaptive learning is clear.

In order to propose the optimal learning activity or material, AI and machine learning's "recommender system" gathers data from all learners in the learning system, keeps track of their prior learning activities, and considers their competency needs. The learning sequence then adjusts to the skill and knowledge level while also adapting to the degree of difficulty of the offered material or questions. Technology and algorithms are used in adaptive learning to provide learners with personalised learning materials. The benefit of adaptive learning strategies is that they reduce the expense and administrative work associated with delivering knowledge through conventional learning techniques.

A chatbot for education may boost productivity, clear up ambiguity in encounters, and increase communication. It achieves the learning outcome by keeping the dialogues brief and concentrating on engagement that is goal-oriented. A chatbot may aid the employee with the lesson planning and use blended learning to deliver learning activities such as tests, games, simulations, and live tutor support to guide the employee through each stage of the process.

To increase the efficiency of the learning process, a conversational interface is used to collect data on user patterns and behaviour. Conversational bots powered by AI can do much more than just talk to one another. Chatbots are employed in dialogue systems for a variety of reasons and are created to realistically mimic how a person acts as a talking partner. Education chatbots help the employee by offering them dynamic, interesting learning content on any subject. Through pictures, voice, or videos, it facilitates their learning and speeds up the examination of their replies to determine how much they have learned.

"Knowledge is a dynamic process that is always changing and evolving; it is no longer just a static piece of information."

Algorithms need data to function. It's crucial to have the ability to turn any data that is gathered into valuable knowledge, though. Speech-to-text and natural learning processes (NLP) can offer practical learning opportunities and support the learning process. Natural learning interactions between employees and learning platforms may be created using NLP. By evaluating material and determining what works and what does not, content analytics paves the way for raising the standard of content. Content analytics provides search engines with more than simply the original content. They help with subject analysis as well as language, phrase, and style analysis of the information being used.

Employing the insights, enterprises may develop intelligent material that is better positioned, flexible, and sensitive to a learner's individual path. Exams, quizzes, and evaluations are becoming significant components of online learning. They support learning consolidation and assess the course's efficacy. These evaluations do, however, have a drawback in that they adopt a one-size-fits-all methodology. Additionally, learning insights contribute to a deeper understanding of learner behaviour and the development of predictive skills. Employing the insights, enterprises may develop intelligent material that is better positioned, flexible, and sensitive to a learner's individual path.

How to retain top talent through the L&D strategy?

During the "Great Resignation", employers that provide their employees with opportunities for growth and development will prosper. However, many businesses still conduct learning programmes using antiquated techniques. Employers who provide chances for employees to upskill and reskill as well as a contemporary perspective on learning and development will prevail. There are several advantages to lifelong learning in the workplace. Effective L&D initiatives, for instance, aid healthcare professionals in comprehending the most recent findings and procedures. Salespeople in the food and beverage business are trained in the most recent safety protocols, and they are skilled at introducing new goods and closing purchases.

The problem is that many HR teams frequently lack the resources necessary to create effective learning programmes that take into account how individuals learn and retain knowledge – resources that are cognizant of how the human brain functions.Too many businesses still use outmoded training techniques like instructor-led training that may be completed online or in person, lengthy SCORM courses, etc. These approaches don't successfully engage workers, help them retain important knowledge, or finally produce the results that contemporary businesses require.

"Learning will only become more stressful for employees if a learning platform is too difficult for them to use."

To minimise employee disruption, learning solutions should be offered inside the established workflow. Employees find it irritating and time-consuming to switch between different systems and manage a list of login details when they are not linked. Businesses should look for microlearning platforms that integrate microlearning into the daily-used programmes that employees currently use, such Slack or Microsoft Teams. This method of employee education boosts output and enables workers to make the connection between what they are learning and their regular duties.

Managers who possess this knowledge can provide those who require it more guidance and learning. Leaders can really help people acquire the vital knowledge they need to perform their jobs by allowing firms to evaluate, modify, and monitor overall learning efficacy. To keep employees content, engaged, and at the organisation, firms' learning and development initiatives must include microlearning heavily. L&D programmes may succeed in pleasing employees and employers and advancing enterprises only when knowledge delivery is based on how the brain remembers information, made easy, and provides business executives with an insight into how effectively knowledge is being kept and used.

As organisations adjust to their new environment, you'll see a wider context for the function of learning and development (L&D) being supplied. Professionals will have the chance to reskill, take advantage of change, and reach their full potential when industries restructure. Most workers have had to adjust to often changing conditions and find their footing in novel and challenging situations over the past two years. The need to manage these changes in the face of a pandemic and the need to reduce new health hazards has necessitated the development of creative techniques to define and achieve milestones. With so much unpredictability, long-term planning has occasionally seemed impossible. In 2020, a sizable portion of the global workforce made the move to remote work, discovering strategies and tools to help them fulfil their in-person responsibilities from in front of a screen.

The future of business as you currently know it will be very different. The year 2021 proceeded in a similar manner, but much of what had been disruptive the year before had now become normal. For instance, the hybrid working model, which most firms pre-pandemic seemed to find unattainable or unfathomable, is now viewed as a progressive goal of forward-thinking, innovative enterprises.

Flexible working numerous organisations at once realised there were many advantages to the disruption once hundreds of millions made the switch to remote work and learning effectively. The realisation that there were several benefits to the transition experience was shared by both the workers and the learners. The changeover was rather simple for authors, graphic designers, web developers, and programmers.

In actuality, more people are choosing to work remotely. People will have to use laptops to work from home starting in 2020. People chose it in 2021. More people than ever before will begin obtaining the necessary skills in 2022 in order to obtain remote employment and take advantage of the advantages it offers.

How can L&D teams negotiate it given that this is occurring both internally and externally?

Let's examine this from the viewpoint of an organisation whose staff successfully made the switch to remote work and is now debating returning to office-based work. They are aware that some of their staff members are more content at home, more productive, better time managers, and all-around more valuable to the organisation.

The solution is obvious when it comes to these two categories of people. hybrid and flexible working methods. Employees that participate in flexible working have greater control over their start and end times, can work whenever they want from home, can compress their workweek (completing five days' worth of work in four), or even share a job. To ensure that the task is completed, there must be a high level of trust between the employer and the employees. On the other hand, hybrid working refers to an organisation's setup through its facilities and digital technology to easily handle a blend of in-person office employees and remote workers, with those people being able to come and go as they please.

There is a lot of training to be done since, according to experts, around 50% of all positions will require upskilling, re-skilling, or cross-skilling to fulfil market demands (or to close the skills gap) in the next two years. new equipment, new ways of working, fresh perspectives, new procedures, new talents, new credentials, and new certificates. Accepting the reality that many ambitious professionals and young executives spend a small sum on the skills they require to join the workforce only to find that the abilities are already outdated is a smart place to start for leadership teams.

To further clarify when an organisation is restructuring yet wants to retain its employees, reskilling refers to learning new skills to transfer into an entirely new career. Employees that are upskilled can provide more value and knowledge to their positions by learning new skills or honing their current ones. It might also be to get them ready for a promotion. Learning new abilities that may be used in several fields to enhance collaboration and assistance is known as cross-skilling. For instance, a salesman may learn graphic design techniques to reduce the workload on the marketing division. This is the time is to invest in human capital and transferable soft skills!

The requirements that an organisation has for its employees are still developing. Hard work, dedication, passion, and devotion are still there, but new factors are beginning to emerge that will influence the next decade. As well as having technological know-how, it will be required that you are creative, compassionate, and resilient. What else is new? Technology is doing what it does best: automating, computing, duplicating, formulating, and optimising processes much more effectively than the typical person. Fortunately, until the singularity, computers won't be able to think like people, which is why transferrable soft skills are so crucial. You are powerful because of who you are as a person. Possess interpersonal skills that have a significant impact on those around you. Think critically and analytically, taking into account a wide range of factors that only you and your thoughts would evaluate, in addition to facts as a machine may.

Digital technology is a major enabler of the revolution. Predictive and advanced analytics, as well as digital technologies, are being used to increase the impact and engagement of learning while also making it genuinely transformative. Recall the days when mentoring was only a quick phone call or meeting at Starbucks? You've depended on a digital mentoring programme to recreate such encounters in our hybrid working style. If a platform is mentee-driven; thus, mentees select their mentors based on algorithm-based suggestions. Many people have chosen mentors from completely different departments or areas. You are ecstatic to see how eager people are to connect and forge relationships throughout the world.

L&D may benefit greatly from the marketing friends they make. Starting with a methodical approach to the business issue you're attempting to resolve is the first step. After that, develop stakeholder personas and their objectives. Prior to your intervention, establish metrics and KPIs so that you are prepared to track, gather, and examine data.

L&D is well-positioned to develop into a hub for connecting people, opportunities, and experiences that help employees succeed and grow throughout time. From onboarding to professional development to departure, L&D will integrate an organisational needs with employee needs, creating pertinent opportunities for people to challenge themselves every day throughout their entire career.

The really strategic L&D leader has finally sat down at the executive table and taken a seat. They have changed their organisation from a vertical, compartmentalised function to one that sits throughout HR. Their team collaborates closely with partners in HR and business to align skill-based personnel development and learning with shared workforce objectives. They encourage people to take charge of their professional growth by giving them the resources and inspiration they need to continue learning throughout their lives.

Additionally, they are aware that improvement begins today, regardless of where they are on their path. When you're prepared to lay out the learning journey, consider carefully how frequently you should communicate with your stakeholders, how to persuade them to click on and view their learning module, and how to get them to ultimately offer the insightful feedback that will help you develop and refine your learning strategy.

According to studies, a sizeable portion of the market value of public firms is dependent on intangible assets, including talented workers, great leaders, and knowledge. These developments have increased the learning and development (L&D) function's significance. L&D executives should invest in training programmes and curriculum development to maximise returns. L&D executives must accept a bigger position within the business and create an ambitious vision for the function in order to maximise investments in training programmes and curriculum development.

To enhance the learning process and results, L&D professionals must keep up with rapidly evolving technology. They must create new learning methodologies and strategies that make use of these advancements, particularly when it comes to AI.

For instance, according to Gartner research, AI-powered chatbots will power 85% of customer care interactions by 2025, while another report claims that 20% of corporate content—including training content—will be created by AI by then. Additionally, according to the Bank of America, economic growth by 2025 would be driven by AI to the tune of $14 to $33 billion yearly. AI will have a significant influence on the L&D sector. Organisations have access to a vast quantity of data that they may evaluate and utilise to enhance their learning curricula.

The days of all employees having to take the same courses are long gone. Content may be tailored to the learner's needs, concentrated on their weaker areas, recommended based on prior behaviour, predicted based on role, and even generated automatically by utilising different content production algorithms. Organisations must harness the massive volumes of data by employing machine learning, data analysts, AI programmers, and more in order to properly leverage AI. The results of this data allow L&D departments to understand the learning journey and assist them in developing training programmes that promote value and support adaptive learning. The creation of learning solutions is influenced by learning styles. Age, race, cultural background, and other elements that must be taken into account during growth may have an impact on a person's learning style.

53% of organisations surveyed by Deloitte ranked the alignment of learning to business outcomes as their top priority. Organisations have been forced to fundamentally rethink the role of learning as a result of the changing business environment and changes brought about by COVID-19, such as remote working and virtualisation. To better integrate learning with business, organisations are developing learning methods. Organisational learning functions are now rethinking how they produce and distribute learning materials as they link learning to an organisational goals as disruptions continue to impact practically every industry.

Virtual delivery is the number one priority for 23% of the organisations polled. Organisations have proven that virtual learning, which is accessible whenever and anywhere, has become the preferred form of education and has shortened the gap between "learning and work." However, there is also a better awareness that each virtual mode should be optimised for the same goals because it is only appropriate for attaining those goals. While just 13% of the organisations polled ranked knowledge management as their top priority, more than 33% of them also included it among their top three concerns.

Virtual learning will make up at least 40% of the formal learning framework, with some organisations anticipating this percentage to reach as high as 90%. Given the occupations, behaviours, habits, and preferences of today's digital learners, it is imperative to make sure learning is interactive, even when virtual learning has become the new standard. The focus of L&D teams has evolved, according to about 62% of executives, to make content 9% "more interactive" through facilitator-led live instructional training, simulations, and panel discussions rather than traditional approaches. In their formal education system, several organisations have adopted LMS as a "course catalogue". About 73% of respondents stated that their organisations already make use of learning management systems. It has historically been used in an organisation for information exchange and internal communication. More than 84% of the organisations said they used Microsoft Teams, OneDrive, and SharePoint frequently for internal communication.

80% of CEOs said they were switching from "content generation" to "content curation," which is more focused and offers information that is more accurate and pertinent at the right moment. This entails offering context-relevant, organised information to the intended audience.This entails offering context-relevant, organised information to the intended audience.

The pool of tacit knowledge held by a department's leaders may be used by L&D departments to curate learner-centered material if they develop effective knowledge management abilities. Approximately 61% of executives think that the shift to personalised content that focuses on the learner is a departure from the conventional learning strategy. This approach is more adapted to the particular requirements of a single employee and, as a result, encourages cooperation and learning in all we do. By focusing on the when, where, and how the work is done, this style of learning offers hyper-personalized learning experiences that are highly contextualised depending on interests, needs, and skills.

"More complex and durable learning come from self-testing, introducing certain difficulties in practice, waiting to re-study new material until a little forgetting has set in, and interleaving the practice of one skill or topic with another." -Peter c. Brown

About 61% of businesses agree that L&D teams must rethink how they encourage a knowledge-sharing ecosystem to assist employees share and transfer their brainpower at work and maximise human potential. They understand that knowledge no longer exists in databases waiting to be retrieved, but rather flows dynamically through digital communication channels that now define working relationships, particularly with the influx of new employees and the departure of seasoned workers. This will help close the gap between formal and casual learning and better contextualise carefully selected learning and development programmes.

On the other hand, one of the main justifications for quitting a firm is a lack of L&D. One of an organisation's most valuable assets is its brand, which communicates a lot about its market performance, financial stability, position in the market, and range of goods and services. Investments in L&D may improve an organisation's reputation as an "employer of choice" and strengthen its brand. Employers must put forth more effort to compete for a limited pool of talent as significant portions of the workforce prepare to retire. They must use an employer value proposition to expressly communicate their brand strength in order to do this. Giving employees the chance to grow and acquire new skills is the most crucial factor in employee engagement. Research reveals that happiness is influenced by lifetime learning. When given the opportunity to grow and develop within their chosen career path, highly engaged individuals are more likely to be inspired by new opportunities at work and satisfied with their current organisation.

Organisations will need to invest more in training as a result of these developments; according to my review data, 60% of respondents intend to raise L&D investment over the next several years, and 66% want to increase the number of staff training hours. Organisations must make sure that the change in the L&D department goes well as they invest more time and resources. The L&D department aids in the implementation of the business plan for many firms. For instance, if a digital transformation is one of the organisation's initiatives, L&D will concentrate on developing the human capital required to make that happen. Every business executive would concur that L&D has to be in line with the broader business goals. However, research has shown that this dimension is often lacking in

L&D functions. Only 40% of businesses claim that their learning strategy is in line with their corporate objectives. Therefore, learning is not explicitly linked to the strategic goals of the organisation for 60% of the population. L&D operations might not be in line with the organisation because of antiquated methods or because budgets were created using criteria from earlier years rather than current imperatives like a digital transformation.

With AI, learning may be accessed online without being tied to a certain location. Create timetables based on when the learner is most productive to improve the effectiveness and efficiency of the learning process. Personal recommendations, tailored assignments, and individual calendars promote greater interest and better engagement. Less stress results in less anxiety and a greater eagerness to learn. The strain on the employee has decreased because rapid explanations are now available by merely putting in a question, bringing personal progress to the forefront. By utilising a variety of AI tools, the academic community is quickly adopting flexible digital and customised learning. The mechanics of how individuals learn have completely changed as a result of easier access to instructional information via computers and smart devices. The future of generating tailored learning experiences for employees is artificial intelligence. Its advantages should not be disregarded.

"You really need to change and think about more productive and sustainable ways to help connect talent to opportunity, and your view is that that's going to be done through a skills-based approach."

Leadership in learning is a crucial component of an organisational culture. The culture of learning you foster will be the force behind transformation in the turbulent, unpredictable, complicated, and ambiguous workplace of today. Although that is a broad mandate, the good news is that you don't have to carry it out on your own. A learning culture is not created from the top down when managers impose the required circumstances and employees play along to comply. It needs a bottom-up strategy with broad support. In order to continuously innovate and complete successful transformation programmes, leaders must enable each employee to become a lifelong learner. People who only feel comfortable doing things one way might not be open to change that causes discomfort. People who have been given this culture of learning are better able to approach problems with intention and a development attitude since they are aware of the advantages that learning experiences have to offer.

Teams may embed the principles of continuous learning through learning via work-based activities, conversation, and use cases where they can see concepts in action, ask questions, and pick the brains of their peers. The problem is that many roadblocks on the transformation path, such as opposition to new procedures, are caused by deeply ingrained behaviours, a lack of proficiency with contemporary working methods, and overall outmoded ways of thinking. The more you think or act in a certain way, the more your brains become accustomed to it and you are more likely to repeat it. However, following the same routine is the exact opposite of transformational.

Organisations may foster ongoing discussion about learning techniques, for instance, by conducting personal evaluations that encourage participants to consider their starting point, establish objectives, and then reflect on their learning journey. This conversation may have an immediate and long-lasting impact on how people learn, think, work, and succeed in teams. An organisational learning and development is a difficult endeavour that necessitates a diverse set of skills. Great learning and development professionals understand instructional design as well as the importance of creating learning cultures within organisations. They can also effectively convey the demands and objectives of learning to executives as well as workers. For seasoned instructional designers and corporate trainers who want to better grasp the function of learning in the workplace and how to successfully lead an organisational learning, this learning path is the next logical step.

Design a learning strategy for an organisation that includes tactics for putting the plan into action, keeping an eye on it, and gauging its success. Create a plan to boost learners' involvement in training programmes and articulate the learning culture for your organisation.

"A learning culture is a business culture that supports systematic, ongoing learning for teams, people, and the entire organisation."

The organisation's overall employee learning agility as well as job engagement will be impacted by the learning culture that is created. Management can use a culture map as a compass to guide corporate culture toward a learning culture. The industrial revolution 4.0 and the VUCCAD world have been ushered in by technological advancements, placing businesses in a constant state of disruption. Organisations must act transformatively if they want to safeguard their sustainable growth. The development of business agility as an organisational adaptable skill is the focus of transformational initiatives.

To create an organisational culture centred on learning, you'll need three things, a friendly learning environment, tangible learning procedures and practises, and leadership that supports learning. You must master three skills: The first step is to provide a secure environment for exploration. Embrace fresh thinking, it is simpler for a team member to offer a fresh approach to solving an issue when employees are aware that you are open to new views and diverse points of view.

- Make room for the unforeseen, while encouraging learning is great, are employees capable of doing so? You don't have to go all-in and embrace Google's well-known 20% guideline in order to let staff members work on their own projects for one day each week. Making sure that the workload permits calmer periods, however, will allow team members to experiment with new concepts, brainstorm, and examine alternate working methods.
- Accept failure (and manage it)! Making errors while experimenting and innovating is also possible. How are you going to take that on board as a part of the process and grow from it
- Concrete learning practices and processes means start incorporating learning into your regular activities right now. Develop learning strategies plans for organisation, team, and individual growth and development are required. For instance, you should include time for learning and development talks when staff receive performance assessments.
- Making an investment in staff development will help facilitate hiring. What training and experience are necessary for employees to advance and become desirable candidates for internal hiring for higher positions? This makes social learning possible. Spending time with others naturally and impulsively leads to the

exchange of knowledge. Nevertheless, you may encourage it by scheduling it.

- Glean an understanding of routine procedures. Do you record project-specific lessons so that teams may apply them to future projects? It is simple to incorporate ideas into the workflow and enhance best practises by storing them in documents that are simple to retrieve. Make sure the procedures, if you're using process documentation, contain steps for recording learning.

- Adding audits ow frequently do you assess the outcomes? Schedule a time to think about the acquired insights after adding process stages. What adjustments are necessary, given what you've learned?

- Leaders must model learning through both their words and deeds if it is to become ingrained in the culture. Sadly, a 2019 Deloitte analysis demonstrates that learning is seldom connected to promotions. Yes, it's simple enough to give learning the lip respect it deserves. However, you must develop a means of recognising learning if you want your staff to take it seriously. Think about the importance you presently place on initiatives for promotions and pay raises, for instance.

- Use of a knowledge base for organisational learning, you need the correct technology basis when promoting an organisational culture that values learning. Organisational silos and technological infrastructure are two of the most prevalent problems, according to a 2020 Deloitte report. A knowledge base is a practical and economical way to keep these problems to a minimum. You may store papers, training materials, and other corporate data in one place by using an internal knowledge base. The knowledge base then supports each stage of organisational learning.

- Collaboration on documentation, note-taking, and the creation of training, procedure, and policy materials. Processes for keeping information should be developed, and best practises should be added.
- Share organisational records and employee training materials, control access, and oversee the onboarding process. A knowledge base is used for both microlearning and macrolearning. The use of an internal knowledge base benefits both macro and micro learning. For instance, Helpjuice provides a Google-like search capability, making it quick and simple for staff members to locate the appropriate knowledge base content.
- Employees may quickly locate the solution in your training materials or documents by searching the knowledge base. A knowledge base can hold complex training or onboarding solutions, including pictures, graphics, and video, for macro learning. Want to demonstrate how you use your project management software to potential hires?
- Simply include a step-by-step instruction manual with screenshots (funny gifs are OK, too!). They can easily access, watch, and replay it as many times as necessary thanks to the knowledge base. A Knowledge Base makes information updates simple. Making changes is simple when using a knowledge base, which is another crucial feature. After all, regular adjustments that come naturally as part of the workflow are essential for an effective organisational learning. For this reason, you should pick a knowledge base with practical editing features.

- Your training materials will always be current, and you won't fear or struggle to implement modifications. An informed base enables you to evaluate how employees use the training. You may also monitor how staff members are utilising the content with a knowledge base that includes analytics and reporting tools.
- The analytics could help you make new decisions about how your company will handle corporate learning. Start your organisation's learning culture off on the right foot. You are aware that the future company's managers' capacity to pick up new information quicker than their rivals will be their only source of competitive advantage. Organisational learning may appear dangerous since it necessitates questioning the current quo, yet it is essential to maintain competitiveness.
- Building the proper culture requires a conducive learning atmosphere, tangible procedures and practises, and leadership that really lives what they preach. With the correct technology base, you'll be prepared to transform an organisational learning from a trendy buzzword to a crucial component of the workplace culture.
- Changing focus from credits to results organisations need to switch from gauging CPEs earned to gauging business results produced in order to start putting lean learning into practise. Lean learning makes sure that workers not only learn the proper material at the appropriate time and for the appropriate purposes but also remember what they have learned.

Corporate culture frequently acts as a barrier or an impediment during the implementation of transformative initiatives rather than as a facilitator. One of the suggested initiatives is to turn corporate culture into a learning culture. An organisation needs to be adaptable if it wants to deal with dynamic changes. Individual, group, and an organisational learning activities foster the development of adaptive capability. These learning activities must be carried out consistently and methodically; they are not irregular or transient.

To be effective, L&D must carefully assess employee competencies and decide which ones are most crucial to assisting in the implementation of the business plan for the organisation. To make sure they are developing a people-capability agenda that actually represents business priorities and strategic objectives, L&D executives should periodically review this alignment. Organisations need to become more flexible and prepared to adjust their business practises and procedures as new tools and technology are continually being developed. Similarly, L&D divisions must be ready to quickly begin capability-building initiatives, for instance, if unexpected business demands materialise or personnel suddenly need instruction in cutting-edge technologies like cloud-based collaboration tools.

By developing a governance framework where leadership from both groups shares responsibility for conceiving, prioritising, planning, and procuring funding for capability-building initiatives, L&D departments may strengthen their collaboration with business executives. There is a lot more to say about instructional strategies, important learning materials, training skills, many types of experimental learning, learning analytics, and other topics. All of these things can not be covered in a whole book.

Your learning and development an organisation may help the an organisation attain the strategic goals set by senior management by employing a carefully designed and rigorously implemented an organisational learning strategy. Learning and development organisations can lose focus and effectiveness when lacking a defined plan. It has been demonstrated that organisations and departments that have experienced agile transformations perform better in operational contexts that are rapidly changing, resulting in higher levels of customer and employee satisfaction, reduced costs, and faster times to market.

Adopting an operating model that allows every component of an organisation or function—its strategy, structure, people, processes, and technology—to become more dynamic while being supported by a strong backbone that ensures efficiency and consistency where necessary, is required for such a transformation. In my opinion, the majority of L&D tasks today are stiff due to their extreme stability. Employees who work in course design, content management, programme delivery, and support for digital platforms may belong to distinct departments with their own key performance indicators that are not always connected to overarching an organisational objectives. For instance, the effectiveness of individuals working in design and development is frequently assessed by the speed with which they can create error-free material and the quantity of learning hours that learners complete, rather than the quality of the learning and its effects.

Instead of any indicator of the level of learning or behavioural change, the major indicators in the delivery of a learning programme are often efficiency (the number of learners in a classroom), employees utilisation, and participant feedback. And rather than the content's applicability to business requirements, content management is measured by how frequently it is updated. These factors make it difficult for L&D staff to work effectively together because they are more concerned with what is important to them than with larger organisational goals and related key performance indicators, such as whether programmes help people get better at their jobs and have a positive business impact. Additionally, L&D personnel may be hesitant to alter tried-and-true procedures even though they are incompatible with next-generation learning.

The reaction time to shifting business demands is slowed down by lengthy, linear project life cycles; huge template libraries with standard operating procedures; and burdensome legacy platforms and systems. The solution to these problems is not total laziness. The talent pool of a corporation is crucial in shaping its culture as a whole. Therefore, it should go without saying that preparing the team for ongoing, incremental change is the most crucial requirement for cultural transformation. An organisation may prepare its human resources for the quick change necessary to succeed in the modern, dynamic business environment by investing in continuous learning. This encourages an environment where people are open to acquiring new, cross-functional abilities.

Without a long-term plan, an L&D department would be aimless, learners would be perplexed if design principles were implemented inconsistently, and an organisation's finances would be at risk in the absence of strict rules for spending and vendor relationships. Stability, for instance, comes with a defined mission, strategy, and budget related to strategic goals to direct the function's work, but the function must also routinely analyse the business's learning requirements so it can constantly realign resources. It needs a more dynamic governance structure to do this, one in which the steering committee meets frequently—possibly quarterly—to discuss money distribution. Assembling the parts that will form a sturdy backbone and the dynamism needed for the function to stay up with an organisation's learning demands will instead help an L&D function find the correct balance between stability and dynamism.

An L&D role similarly requires a strong team of specialists in disciplines including experience design, multichannel distribution, curation, and analytics. These areas will be of great use to the function and an organisation's work. However, there should also be a "flow to work" pool of resources that can quickly fill in for priorities as needed; for instance, a team of instructional designers that can assist various business units and operate across various topic areas. Importantly, employees of the L&D team frequently participate in cross-functional project teams with end-to-end ownership and decision-making power, which are essential components of an agile operation that aims to produce quickly. The role will also need to continually upgrade its skill profile in order to remain relevant.

An agile transformation's success is defined by (that is, by making explicit the goal of both efficiency—for example, the time it takes to generate a learning asset—and improved business performance). Everyone is aware of what success will entail. Understanding what cutting-edge techniques may do is crucial since the objective should be aspirational. To ensure that L&D remains focused on generating value, it is crucial that business executives contribute to setting the goal. an organisational differences will affect how long it takes to convert an L&D function and the steps that must be taken. Depending on the starting point, complexity, intended pace, and audacity of an organisation. However, the majority of transformations need well preparation.

A successful agile transformation is characterised by the establishment of an L&D "North Star" related to an organisation's strategic goals. Everyone is aware of what success will entail. The objective should be challenging, so it's critical to know what cutting-edge techniques can do. To ensure that L&D remains focused on generating value, it is crucial that business executives contribute to setting the goal. Evaluate the starting location. The right actions and priorities may be chosen if an L&D function's present skills and readiness for change are honestly assessed. The assessment should encompass previously mentioned criteria plus feedback from learning specialists, end users, and business executives.

Organisations can set goals and priorities by using "performance grids" to assess how their L&D functions compare to best practises. They create the operating system and the future course. An organisation may organise its L&D function's structure, methods, and necessary capabilities; set a budget; and choose initiatives and their sequencing if it has a clear grasp of a starting point. If an organisation is transitioning in response to automation and new market prospects, large-scale reskilling may be necessary. It's crucial to start with these projects while including fast wins to keep the momentum going. These might be continuing initiatives, like those for onboarding and leadership development, or trial projects to switch to a digital customer-service model inside certain business sectors.

Implementation is an iterative process, as with any agile transformation. Some businesses could decide to completely overhaul their L&D operations from the start, preparing to put up with the anticipated short-term interruptions in exchange for a quicker transition. However, the majority begin with one or more pilots and learn from them before spreading the new methods of operation. In either case, ongoing development is critical. The strategy and operational models of L&D departments must adapt as the organisation and external surroundings do. Although leadership must be learner-oriented, it cannot be restricted to the top levels. In one instance, a large corporation began its cultural change by focusing on senior executives' leadership development. The programme was subsequently modified and scaled across the board, sending a message about the significance of learning for people and teams at all levels.

Open knowledge platforms may engage employees, enabling them to exchange and access information and discover new opportunities for innovation. Technology, especially digital learning, will play a significant role in expanding education and gathering information that will enable businesses to constantly increase their efforts. Human ties are equally vital. These relationships provide a network that gives workers the chance to learn from one another and increase psychological safety throughout the organisation.

Make a setting for learning that encourages reskilling. Learning is a creative discipline that calls for a balance of classroom instruction and real-world experience, as well as room for inquiry. Curiosity motivates people to learn new things and encourages experimentation, including reskilling. Over 87% of CEOs say their organisation has a skills gap. By fostering an atmosphere where individuals may "learn to earn" and develop more adaptability and resilience, these issues can be effectively addressed.

Organisations are better prepared for anticipated future role disruption by just starting reskilling programs—rather than waiting. Begin today, do your tests quickly, and iterate. This book is a part of your organisational transformation that investigates a new set of ideas, including experimentation and anti-fragility, that are becoming more and more important for today's businesses as they create more innovative, adaptive, and human systems. Learning and development have a responsibility to become their best selves at a time of great change. Learning leaders are breaking through old silos as a result of the transformation of learning and development (L&D) in order to work together on a more comprehensive vision for HR. While simultaneously bringing a new sense of care and compassion to employee well-being, diversity, and inclusion, they are searching for novel ways that relate skill development to career paths, internal mobility, and retention.

L&D is now more strategically important, cross-functional, and overworked. Over the past two years, learning leaders have met and exceeded high expectations. They are only getting started in the spotlight, but one thing is certain. The majority of L&D leaders—nearly three-fourths—agree that L&D has gained more influence in the past year. It's a huge task to manage the increased duties that come with a changing position. And L&D professionals are grabbing the chance to take the lead, whether it is by assisting their businesses in adapting to change or in reinventing the future. To maintain leadership, they must now choose how to prioritise their tasks.

Learning leaders made it clear that their workload for 2022 is excessive. The number of replies for each programme I tracked grew year over year when I compared this year's findings to the previous year's (either significantly or directionally). The creation of impactful, high-caliber learning experiences is the responsibility of learning leaders. However, they are also dealing with broader, more complex issues, including future-proofing their organisations. This requires learning new techniques and methods of working as well as careful prioritising.

The need for time for personal learning has decreased as L&D's to-do lists have grown exponentially. It's never easy to find time to learn. However, there is a new sense of urgency. Although learning leaders have made several adjustments, it is obvious that more has to be done. Organisations may get ready for and lessen disruption in the future by taking positive steps and adopting a learning attitude. Leaders are being pushed to get ready for unprecedented organisational transformation by the anticipation of a post-pandemic future and the rising demand for the cutting-edge skillsets required for employment in the future. In my opinion, accelerated learning is imperatives that are essential for preparing for the future. If accelerated learning is successfully implemented, benefits include increased creativity, expanded capacities, and the capacity for real-time skill upgrading.

The inclination to concentrate on what you already know is a barrier to learning that frequently prevents organisations and learners from progressing. Instead of asking yourselves, "What do I need to learn to develop myself and deliver?" most individuals spend their time in performance mode, attempting to prove that "This is what I know and this is my competence." You must learn how to learn in order to counteract this. Learning is a muscle that can be developed, flexed, and strengthened. Doing so will help people learn more rapidly, adjust to change more successfully, and develop resilience. No matter how much experience a person has, success in continual learning is predicted by flexibility and resilience. These characteristics are crucial design requirements for learning systems as well; they describe the ecology and environment that an organisation creates for learning and reskilling. How then, do businesses and executives speed learning while preparing their teams for the future? These three things can open doors.

Develop a mindset that is open to learning at all levels. Businesses should support employees in embracing experimentation, risk, and surprise on an individual, team, and an organisational level. The majority of learning comes from testing new theories and assumptions while working. But for such learning to be effective, organisations must provide a space where employees may draw lessons from both achievements and mistakes, both their own and those of others. Processes, codified structures like feedback loops, as well as cultural components like psychological safety, might assist in bringing about change in this situation.

Make your organisation's learning and development plan a top focus. Senior management should be given sufficient funding, resources, and support to advance their professional growth. Examples of such officers are corporate learning officers and education executives. One of the top goals must be the senior management officials' career development. To produce effective corporate training materials and leadership development programmes, incorporate resource utilisation concerns into your learning and development plan.

In conclusion, the shift to remote or online employment is less driven by the epidemic situation and more driven by personal goals and chosen working methods. People want to enhance their professions, improve their skill sets, and work more flexibly all at once. In 2022, L&D specialists and technologies that can combine these three goals will prevail. The second trend is the increase in cross-skilling, upskilling, and reskilling. Many restaurants are closing because they lack workers.

"People today take responsibility for their own personal and professional growth and development, which is one of the reasons opportunities for learning and development are listed as one of the top requirements for employment"
- Dr. Amit Das

References

- *The Learning & Development Book: Change the way you think about L & D by Tricia Emerson , Mary Stewart Format: Kindle Edition 2012.*
- *Psychology Of Learning And Development Paperback – January 2019 by Mangal S. K. , Mangal Shubhra.*
- *Learning and Development: From Cost Center to Business Partner Mass Market Paperback – July 2020 by Zubin Rashid.*
- *A Practical Guide for Behavioural Leadership: Embedding organisational learning for high performance using the MILL model Hardcover –December 2017 by Arjan Molenkamp.*
- *Organizational Learning from Performance Feedback: A Behavioral Perspective on Innovation and Change Hardcover – June 2003 by Hentrich R. Greve.*
- *Organisational Learning and Effectiveness Paperback – 22 October 1998 by Denton John.*
- *Organisational learning and development during a recession: How eBay, Apple and Google foster organisational learning and development Kindle Edition by Marianne Reyes, June 2011.*
- *Learning and Organisational Development Essentials, Graham Willard by, March 2020.*
- *Organisational Learning and its Effectiveness, November 2016 by Ashraf Ali Sarfaraz.*
- *Organisational Learning: An integrated HR and knowledge management perspective Paperback- May 2016 by Roderick Smith.*
- *The Connector Manager: Why Some Leaders Build*

Exceptional Talent – and Others Don't by Jaime Roca and Sari Wilde, September 2011.

- *Neuroscience for Learning and Development: How to Apply Neuroscience and Psychology for Improved Learning and Training 2nd Edition* by Stella Collins, Aug 2019.
- *Hidden Talents: Practical Tools and Inspirational Stories to Unleash Higher Levels of Leadership Performance Kindle Edition* by Maryanne DiMarzo (Author), Amy Acker (Author), & 1 more Format: Kindle Edition, Oct 2019.
- *Creating Significant Learning Experiences: An Integrated Approach to Designing College Courses Revised and Updated Edition* by L. Dee Fink (Author), Aug 2013.
- *How to Be an Inclusive Leader: Your Role in Creating Cultures of Belonging Where Everyone Can Thrive Hardcover – August 20, 2019* by Jennifer Brown.
- *Agile Transformation: Structures, Processes and Mindsets for the Digital Age 1st Edition* by Neil Perkin, Oct 2019.
- *Bet on Talent: How to Create a Remarkable Culture That Wins the Hearts of Customers Hardcover – September 3, 2019* by Dee Ann Turner (Author), Patrick Lencioni (Foreword).
- *e-Learning and the Science of Instruction: Proven Guidelines for Consumers and Designers of Multimedia Learning 3rd Edition* by Ruth C. Clark, Richard E. Mayer , Aug 2011.
- *The Adult Learner: The definitive classic in adult education and human resource development 8th Edition* by Malcolm S. Knowles , Elwood F. Holton III, Richard A. Swanson , Jan 2015.
- *Adult Learning: Linking Theory and Practice* by Sharan B. Merriam,Laura L. Bierema, Oct 2013.
- *How We Learn: The Surprising Truth About When, Where, and Why It Happens Paperback – June 9, 2015* by

Benedict Carey.

- *Make It Stick: The Science of Successful Learning Hardcover – April 14, 2014 by Peter C. Brown , Henry L. Roediger III , Mark A. McDaniel .*
- *Telling Ain't Training: Updated, Expanded, Enhanced Paperback – June 16, 2011by Harold D. Stolovitch , Erica J. Keeps.*
- *The Art and Science of Training Paperback – December 15, 2016 by Elaine Biech.*
- *Design for How People Learn (Voices That Matter) 2nd Edition by Julie Dirksen , Dec 2015.*
- *Brilliance by Design: Creating Learning Experiences That Connect, Inspire, and Engage Paperback – Illustrated, January 10, 2011 by Vicki Halsey.*
- *Learning Technologies in the Workplace: How to Successfully Implement Learning Technologies in Organizations 1st Edition by Donald H Taylor, Sep 2017.*
- *LMS Success: A Step-by-Step Guide to Learning Management System Administration 2nd Edition by Katrina Marie Baker, April 2018.*
- *The Feedback Imperative: How to Give Everyday Feedback to Speed Up Your Team's Success Paperback – June 17, 2014 by Anna Carroll.*
- *The 5 Languages of Appreciation in the Workplace: Empowering Organizations by Encouraging People Paperback – September 1, 2012 by Gary Chapman , Paul White.*
- *The Gamification of Learning and Instruction: Game-based Methods and Strategies for Training and Education 1st Edition by Karl M. Kapp, May 2012.*
- *Actionable Gamification: Beyond Points, Badges and Leaderboards Paperback – April 14, 2015 by Yu-kai Chou.*
- *1501 Ways to Reward Employees Paperback – March 27,*

2012 by Bob B. Nelson.

- *Optimizing Talent: What Every Leader and Manager Needs to Know to Sustain the Ultimate Workforce (Hc) (Contemporary Trends in Organization Development and Change) Hardcover – October 29, 2010 by Linda Sharkey , Paul H. Eccher.*
- *The Six Disciplines of Breakthrough Learning: How to Turn Training and Development into Business Results 3rd Edition by Roy V. H. Pollock (Author), Andy Jefferson (Author), Calhoun W. Wick (Author), Dec 2017*
- *Transferring Learning to Behavior: Using the Four Levels to Improve Performance Hardcover – March 10, 2005 by Donald L. Kirkpatrick (Author), James D. Kirkpatrick (Author)*
- *Seven Trends in Corporate Training and Development: Strategies to Align Goals With Employee Needs (FT Press Human Resources) 1st Edition by Ibraiz Tarique , May 2014.*
- *Minds at Work: Managing for Success in the Knowledge Economy Paperback – December 7, 2017 by David Grebow , Stephen J. Gill.*
- *Managers As Mentors: Building Partnerships for Learning Paperback – June, 2013 by Chip R. Bell.*
- *Make Talent Your Business: How Exceptional Managers Develop People While Getting Results Paperback – May , 2011 by Wendy Axelrod , Jeannie Coyl.*
- *Employee Development on a Shoestring Paperback – April, 2012 by Halelly Azulay.*
- *Engaging the Online Learner: Activities and Resources for Creative Instruction Updated Edition by Rita-Marie Conrad , J. Ana Donaldson, May 2011.*
- *Bridging the Soft Skills Gap: How to Teach the Missing Basics to Todays Young Talent Hardcover – September ,*

2015 by Bruce Tulgan.

About The Author

Dr. Amit Das, is a renowned executive advisor, consultant, educationist, author, speaker, counsellor, and coach whose 25+ years of business experience provides high-impact, practical solutions that support his clients' leadership development and organisational transformations. He worked for fortune 500 MNCs and left rich leagacy of organising transformational learning workshops. He has transformed more than 5000+ working executives through his path breaking capability building learning workshops. Dr. Amit Das is recognised as an innovative, principled thought leader who combines intellectual rigor and discipline with an ability to translate theory into practice. His operational skills are coupled with a strategic ability to analyse, develop, and implement successful strategies for profitability, growth, and sustainability.

Dr. Amit Das has a successful track record in aligning learning and training solutions to key business strategy with a strong focus on flawless execution excellence to facilitate individual, business divisional, and organisational performance. He keeps relentless focus on measuring training impact and ROI, people capability building graphs, training process governance, performance coaching, and strategic thinking. These have been some of his key individual success traits. His core capabilities include performance coaching, designing training and development frameworks, psychometric assessment and analysis, competency framework development and assessments, content design and facilitation of soft skills and leadership programmes, Learning Management Systems, Learning Impact Measurement, Talent Analysis, and Performance Coaching and Counselling.

Dr. Amit Das has authored multiple management and self-development books, like Create Your Leadership Edge, Building Organisational Capability, Ethical Road Map, Attomic Attention, BYPB, Implementor, ALOUD, Redefining Talent Management, Defining Your Success Factors, Lead or Plead, Make The Most Of Your Life, Better Half or Bitter Half, The Transformative Mind & Soul are few of them.

He has a Ph.D. and a Fellowship in strategic learning, along with his first class degrees in Human Resource Management, Marketing Management, International Business, and Corporate Laws from the top business schools in India. He is a certified Psychometric analyst, HR Analyst, OD Interventionist, Human Psychologist, Lifecoach, Leadership Developer, Black Belt (LSS), Strategic Thinker, Talent Analyst, certified professional trainer from the U.K. and certified behavioral coach from the U.S.A.

Dr. Amit Das likes googling, reading books, writing articles & books, cooking, listening to old melodies, and counselling people to unleash their true potential to build a strong nation. He is married and blessed with a son. He would love to hear about your experience after reading his books. You can email him and share your thoughts, or you can use his services for life coaching, positive behavioural counseling, educational support, and mentoring for young, promising students pursuing their B.B.A. and M.B.A. degrees.

www.ingramcontent.com/pod-product-compliance
Lightning Source LLC
Chambersburg PA
CBHW031623170726
47990CB00016B/344